Foreword

For the best part of four years, Keith Graham has joined me each Friday on my daily Radio Scotland programme, Macgregor's Gathering. We talk about Scottish wildlife, and he has proved to be a genial and stimulating colleague. He is a naturally concientious and meticulous worker, and arrives punctually at the studio with a carefully prepared script. So infectious is his enthusiasm, however, that our conversation usually takes off unbidden, and the script is virtually ignored. The technique, or lack of it, appears to be effective, for Keith's guest spot is one of the best established on the programme, and brings in a heavy and enthusiastic mail from the listeners.

We have made several outdoor expeditions together; some for radio, some for television, some for just the crack, and Keith always demonstrates a keen eye and ear, as well as a deeply felt concern for the natural world. Keith Graham's writing style exactly matches his approach to broadcasting. He is well informed and enthusiastic and informal, and this little collection of essays demonstrates once again that he is a natural and highly effective communicator.

Jimmie Macgregor

Jimmie Macgregor

COUNTRY VIEW

Keith Graham

Illustrated by
Arthur Ingham

This second collection of my "Country View" articles in the 'Stirling Observer'
has given me special delight because not only does it give my weekly
wildlife column a kind of permanence but it has also brought me into contact
with Arthur Ingham. His sensitive illustrations have, I believe, added a new
dimension to my writing.
I am grateful to Scottish & Universal Newspapers for showing enthusiasm for
the collection and especially to Alan Rennie the editor of the
'Stirling Observer' and his staff.
I sincerely thank The John Jamieson Munro Trust and its administrators,
without whose help this book could not have been published.

Published by:
Scottish & Universal Newspapers Ltd.
36 Tay Street, Perth PH1 5TT
and 40 Craigs, Stirling FK8 2DW

Distributed by:
Clan Books, The Cross, Doune,
Perthshire FK16 6BE

January
February
March

A touch of colour

THE thin blanket of snow combined with a distinctly grey sky to give the landscape a monochrome appearance almost devoid of colour, bleak and, with the accompaniment of a snell easterly draught; not too warm either.

The monotone quality of the scene was in some ways accentuated by the flat white surface of the loch — a crust of snow lying on the inch or two of ice now covering the whole surface — save for a few square yards of now ruffled water in one corner where the remaining wildfowl have presumably kept the water sufficiently stirred to prevent a total freeze.

Yet, even this tiny oasis was slowly falling victim to the advance of the ice. Mini ice floes provided floating rafts upon which huddled groups of mallard and coot.

As I made my way towards this last unfrozen encampment for the normally healthy winter population of water-fowl across frozen fields just covered with snow, I realised I was following in the footsteps of dozens of rabbits, their passage marked by patterned imprints in the snow.

The dry, dead leaves of thistles rattled in the cutting wind, solitary monuments to a summer long past and consigned to the scrapbook.

A small plantation gave me sheltered respite from the coldness of the breeze and, of more importance, allowed me to approach this 'water hole' unseen by its occupants.

At last I was close enough to survey the scene in more detail. Two mute swans stood on the ice but at the very edge of the broken water. And bobbing about in that ruffled pool were about three dozen coot, even now, in the depths of winter, maintaining a degree of their traditional aggression as male chased male from minuscule territory.

Coot always look as if they are hunched up . . . and these had good cause to look even more hunched up than usual; I dared not think of the temperature of the water in which they were idly paddling.

There was, inevitably, a sprinkling of mallard, some roosting — on one leg — in a line along their artificial icy shoreline, some resting on the beach against which the tiny waves of this small pool lapped.

Others indulged themselves in the luxury of this last watery haven by tipping up and guddling. A pair of teal stood on one of the mini ice floes, a picture of boredom!

There were a few tufted duck too, the drakes notably sporting splendid 'quiffs' as if to underline their appropriate titling;

and one solitary pink-footed goose, its head and upper neck dark, waddling along that same icy strand, giving the impression of passing the time of day with the roosting mallard with which it communed.

A movement caught my eye away to the right along the wooded shore beyond a magnificent group of Scots pine.

Out on to the ice he strolled, tentatively at first but then with added confidence as he realised that the ice was comfortably bearing his weight. Across this white expanse he padded, an adventurer in territory as alien as it could possibly be. Not too many foxes extend their hunting territory to encompass the surface of a loch!

His appearance certainly disturbed the two swans. First they waddled clumsily along the edge of the pool, then they slid easily into the dark waters.

He padded on with an air of disinterest but they were not prepared to stay to see if he would approach this tiny refuge. As one they suddenly began to taxi across the water, paddling furiously with those large, black, webbed feet until they were airborn, literally whistling into the wind.

Away they sailed like two huge airborn yachts. I could still hear those whistling wingbeats long after they had disappeared from view round the wooded headland.

He stopped to watch their departure. There was no sign of apprehension in his posture. He just seemed to be an interested spectator. He travelled further to where a scattering of droppings indicated that this had been a fairly substantial roost during the night — probably the now departed colleagues of my one solitary pink-foot.

He sniffed here and there but, realising that the birds had long since flown, turned on his heels and re-traced his steps back to the woodland from which he had emerged.

There was enough distance between the fox and the pool for there to be little or no immediate threat to the remaining occupants. At least they seemed unconcerned and he disinterested in their presence.

Some of the coot were now coming ashore perhaps tired of searching rather fruitlessly for food in their pool, picking here and there at the dry grass seeds — a morsel here and a morsel there.

Just above them sat a lone rabbit on top of the shallow bank, assiduously washing its face and generally having something of a brush-up.

Suddenly, some of the coot scattered, more in surprise than panic. Through their midst bounded a grey squirrel, departing the young plantation and heading for the birch and Scots pine.

I say bounded because, as he raced away from me, he seemed to have springs in those splayed rear limbs. Halfway across the treeless shore, he stopped, seemed to look at the rabbit, stood bolt upright, sifting the air, and then re-commenced his spring heeled passage towards the more familiar trees.

A flurry of fieldfares descended noisily on the beach but only for a moment or two before just as noisily removing themselves to somewhere, presumably, a little more profitable.

The coot came and went to and from the water, it seemed, almost in relays. The mallard preened and guddled, tufties swam and plopped periodically under the surface, the lone goose waddled ashore and picked at the grass and the rabbit sat . . . and sat . . . and sat.

When at last I left them to their own devices, I briefly communed with a racing snipe as it darted almost from under my feet and zig-zagged away before plummeting into a reed bed.

It was not, after all, such a monochrome day!

Translating birdsong into names

IF we did not enjoy a white Christmas — if "enjoy" is the right word — those who celebrate the 'Old Christmas' during the month of January, seem destined to do so with a seasonal covering of snow.

Indeed the arrival of snow just a day or two into the New Year, has inevitably begun to change the patterns of movements of the birds. The great skeins of geese which herald each morning for me and the softer fluting of the whoopers, has receded, if only slightly, as these visitors from the far north disperse a little farther in their search for food.

My bird table is now much more active too with many more finches taking advantage of the bird seed now that the plentiful surplus of grain in the surrounding fields is to all intents and purposes, locked up by the snow and ice.

Most of the broad billed visitors are chaffinches and greenfinches, the cock birds resplendent in their colourful winter plumage. Although chaffinches are perhaps one of the commonest of birds in this part of Scotland, they are no less attractive for that. There are indeed few more colourful birds with the male's bright pink breast, his delightful slate grey head and chestnut coloured back. In flight, a greenish rump is shown and there are two bold white flashes offset by tinges of yellow on the wings.

As is the case in so many birds, it is the cock that boasts the colourful clothes for the female is plain by contrast.

The fact that chaffinches are so widespread and thus so familiar has given rise to a whole catalogue of nicknames. Francesca Greenoak in her splendid book, "All the Birds in the Air," lists no fewer than 43 colloquial names, the most familiar of which, locally at least, is probably 'Shelfie.' However, some readers may use the name, 'Wet Bird,' attributed to the County of Stirling but one, I must confess, I have never heard in conversation.

Many such names of course derive from particular features of a bird's plumage. It comes therefore as little surprise, that the chaffinch is known by the title, 'Blue Cap' as 'White Wingie' and 'Fleckiwing' in various parts of Scotland.

Similarly, the familiar 'pink, pink' call also gives rise to such names as 'Binkie,' 'Chy' and 'Prink, Prink.' Another name, 'Boldie' — in this case, from Kincardine — is perhaps derived from the fact that chaffinches are by nature much less shy than most other birds and as opportunists, have found that living cheek by jowl with man, can often be profitable.

Visit most picnic areas in the summer and you will find yourself watching chaffinches scavenging the crumbs from your picnic with the greatest of glee!

The other extremely familiar facet of chaffinch life is that vigorous and tuneful song . . . always a welcome sound as spring approaches and, in my view, as much a heralding of spring as any other sound of the countryside. The poet, William Allingham interpreted the cheery song thus:—

'Sweet, sweet, sweet.
Pretty lovely, come and meet me here.'

In this particular case, the translation of the song into human language is particularly appropriate for that is precisely the object of the exercise — to attract a suitable female to share a territory and . . . the nuptials!

In most gardens, the greenfinch is no less familiar and, I am sure, a bird well recognised for its aggressive behaviour round a bird table. Greenfinches and chaffinches form substantial marauding flocks during the winter, often with the added company of a sprinkling of yellowhammers. This autumn and winter seems to have seen even larger flocks of them than usual, almost certainly because of the exceptional amount of spilt grain in the fields.

Like chaffinches, greenfinches are more than happy to exploit man-made habitats and prepared therefore to live cheek by jowl with us. It is therefore surprising to note that they lack the range of colloquial names. Miss Greenoak records a paltry nine names.

In fact it was the local use of one of these names which prompted me to reach for Francesca Greenoak's book. A local farmer's wife referred to a flock of greenfinches by the title, 'Peasweeps'!

Such a reference immediately prompted in my mind, thoughts of lapwings, now much confined to coastal areas and indeed such names as 'Peesweep' (note the different spelling which is, I suppose, meaningless in terms of the spoken word) and 'Peesieweep' are probably more familar to many folk than the bird's proper name.

'Peasweep' as a name for a greenfinch is, like the colloquialism for the lapwing, entirely related to the long drawn out note uttered by greenfinches — a note which resembles a chesty wheeze!

'Green Linnet' is a familiar name for greenfinches too and that they resemble linnets in shape and size, easily accounts for such a name. Pleasant though the musical twittering of greenfinches can be, it would be a gross insult to linnets to even begin to compare the two songs.

With the hardening of the weather, now is the time we might expect to see other, less familiar finches joining in the general melee to find food. Close to areas with pine plantations, siskins are becoming an increasingly familar sight on bird tables.

The flashes of yellow on the much darker wings are particularly noticeable — two of them. But in general, the siskin is much more heavily marked and generally darker than the greenfinch. And the male birds possess a handsome grey crown.

More like the chaffinch is the brightly coloured brambling, a visitor from the north in winter time. The colour combination is similar to that of a chaffinch but the breast colouration tends more to orange than pink. The white wing flashes are also rather less prominent in the brambling and there is extra colour on the wings with two orange patches on the inner leading edges. Most noticeable is the bold white rump flash when the bird flies and there is also rather heavier marking.

Other occasional visitors in harder weather may include the heavily billed hawfinch — again not dissimilar in colouring from the chaffinch — the bullfinch with its squatter shape and very noticeable white rump and the brilliantly coloured goldfinch with its red face and marvellous flashes of gold or yellow.

And especially in the more urban areas, the most remarkable visitors of all, the waxwing, also a visitor from the far north.

Bigger than the finches, here is a striking bird with its chestnut coloured head, surmounted by a fine crest, black chin and, the feature that gives this bird its name, the remarkable wax like red tips to the upper flight feathers which add a curious embellishment to the otherwise black, yellow and white wings.

And with such an outstandingly individual appearance and a name to match it, who needs a local name for that?

Houdini story

WITHOUT a doubt, the most outstanding individual memory I have of the old year is the incredible survival story of Houdini.

This is a story of a tawny owl caught up in fishing line over one of our rivers . . . fishing line, I might say, very carelessly — and thoughtlessly — left hanging from the branches of the trees which line the bank of that particular stretch of river.

I had no way of telling just how long the owl had been thus stranded but as I patiently cut away the yards of line wrapped round and round the wing, by which the poor bird had been helplessly suspended, it became apparent that the unintentional trap had imprisoned the unwitting owl for some time . . . I judged at least forty eight hours.

In untangling the masses of nylon line, I had also to cut the main flight feathers on the wing. So flight for the bird would be out of the question for some time — at least until the annual moult towards the end of summer.

The incident happened in May and, for a few days, I duly kept the owl in close confinement, providing as much food each day, as it would eat.

It soon became obvious, however, that our rescue had come too late for the beast. The strangulation of the blood supply in the wing caused permanent damage and, within a few days, de-generation had set in and part of the wing eventually detached itself to leave this particular owl effectively flightless for the rest of its life.

Worse was to follow! At no time during its confinement was the captive owl anything other than aggressive and very wild. Indeed so badly did it take to captivity that it decided to return to the wild and duly escaped.

In spite of extensive searches in the surrounding fields and woodlands, I could find no trace at all of the escapee and sadly concluded, after about a week, that it must have perished.

Imagine my surprise, therefore, when some seven weeks later, the bird turned up in my orchard. There it was one morning, perched nonchalantly near the top of one of the old damson trees.

How it had survived for almost two months, baffles me, save to say that like many birds of prey, tawny owls, when they have to, are quite prepared to eat earthworms and other insects when other food is scarce.

And it also seemed just possible that the exceptional night vision of this tawny might also enable it to take the odd roosting bird from the surrounding trees.

But there it was, as large as life, perched in the trees in my orchard and there it has remained.

Now it finds life rather easier for each morning, food is especially put out for it. And, each morning, Houdini (what else could I have called it?) clambers down through the branches, feasts, and then returns to its lofty perch.

On occasions, Houdini flutters to the ground to devour the food thus provided, using the stump of a wing to keep balance. He never seems to land on anything but his feet albeit somewhat clumsily. And, in due course, Houdini then returns to a perch by literally climbing up one of the trees.

During the summer and autumn, it was pretty difficult to spot him amongst the foliage and even now, with the branches naked, I am treated to an exercise in aninmal . . . or bird . . . camouflage. In fact, there are mornings when I simply cannot find him.

On other occasions, I eventually trace him with some difficulty for when perched close to a main branch or the trunk, with plumage held tight to the body, eyes reduced to malevolent slits and a coloration so like the colour of the tree bark, Houdini literally merges perfectly with the background.

And the chosen perch differs each day. When the weather is coming from the west, a perch on the eastern side of the trunk is chosen. The worse the weather, the closer in to the main tree trunk is the roosting place.

Houdini's story is a remarkable saga which illustrates most vividly the strong survival instinct of some creatures. That this particular owl may never again float on silent wings to pounce on some hapless vole or mouse, is evident: some would say, sad.

But, in spite of a disability which would see off most other birds, this particular owl is able to live something akin to a normal life. In fact, I suppose as long as I feed it, it will remain a permanent resident, who knows, perhaps for years!

I have no doubt that there have been more dramatic survival stories . . . and that there will be much more dramatic survivals.

Nature, thank God, is resilient. She has to be for man, the most advanced form of life, constantly puts nature under pressure. Each day, somewhere in the world, several species of wildlife are lost . . . for ever. Someone has actually calculated that a species dies out every few minutes of every day.

That raw fact may not seem to be especially important in the face of man's drive for greater and greater wealth. Economics seem now to dominate every aspect of life at the expense of most other considerations. We do not, in my view, take our responsibility for the other resources of this planet seriously enough.

Maybe there is a moving tide of opinion slowly gathering which demands that we care more for the world we live in. I hope so, for any other road taken can only result in our own eventual demise as a species.

Throughout the nineteen eighties, a better climate of awareness has been developing, yet we still do some incredibly stupid things.

In world terms, we continue to destroy the rain forests of South America. In national terms, we in Britain continue to provide Scandinavia with our most unwelcome export — acid rain.

On the Isle of Islay, the future of a substantial percentage of the world's population of Greenland white fronted geese, seems threatened by the exploitation of the peat moss upon which they winter . . . in spite of advice given to the authorities by the Nature Conservancy Council and in spite of the fact that there is so much more peat on Islay which could be extracted for the use of the whisky distillers.

As the second half of the eighties gets under way I pray for rather more concern and common sense to be displayed by those charged with the responsibility for our environment. If they respond to that challenge, then this will indeed be a happier New Year!

Tawny Owl

Signs of Spring but Winter holds on

THE North Sea roared in on the shingly beach, its green waves surmounted by white foaming crests, crashing on to the stones.

Off shore a fleet of fishing boats lurched towards the calmer waters of the harbour, their success marked by the milling flocks of gulls plundering the unwanted 'innards'.

But above the roaring of the furious waves there rose the shrill chanting of a posse of oyster-catchers.

They too plundered but their 'catches' were much smaller fry; worms and shrimps, insects and other such goodies.

Oyster-catchers

They scampered, as only oyster-catchers can, in erratic fashion, always pausing to give voice, in defiance, it seemed, of the crashing waves.

They reminded me that the Day of St. Bride has passed. Not that such an event is of much significance these days, for many of the ancient festivals are disappearing, in this case not even recorded in my diary.

In place of "The Day of Bride" it now reads "PAYE week 44"! How dull!

To our Celtic ancestors, that day, February 1, had considerable significance. On St. Bride's Day, spring was heralded in . . . notably by the high pitched calling of the Saint's very own bird, that same oyster-catcher, better known as Ghillie Bride.

Well, it hasn't felt very much like spring yet. Furthermore I was reminded of the 'each way' bet that the winter is only halfway through!

Apparently tradition has it that it is good farming practice to have only exhausted half of one's winter keep — hay — by Candlemas, which, as it happens, falls on the day after St. Bride's Festival.

By implication, I have to assume that there is plenty of hay feeding ahead of us.

And yet, there are odd days borrowed from spring. A week ago, larks were singing high above as I went about my early morning chores. I've seen little bands of curlews on preliminary skir-mishes inland and a few flocks of lapwing too.

But like our Celtic ancestors, I never believe that spring has really arrived until I hear those noisy, shrill pipings of Ghillie Bride.

When they arrive in the fields to prod with their orange beaks for the store of hidden delicacies — worms, leather-jackets and the like — then and only then, will I believe that winter is in full retreat.

My short-lived expedition to the sea-shore at least reminded me of what is to come and nurtures in my breast a feeling of expectation.

When will the oyster-catchers' shrill notes echo from the fields? How long before the lapwings begin their wonder-ful aerial dancing to celebrate the great season of passion? When might I expect that lyrical call of the whaup to embellish the hillside?

Patience is a virtue. All in good time.

Only when the frosts have loosened their grip will these birds grace us with their presence, for to survive, they must probe the ground — each at a different level — for the millions of unseen beasties that lurk below the turf.

The curlews with their long curved bills, dig deepest, then comes the oyster-catcher, shopping at a higher level. Finally the peewit seeks out its daily bread just below the surface. Thus all can share the same piece of ground without actually competing with each other.

They survive the winter by repairing to the coasts and estuaries where the mud or sand is always yielding; where they can prod to their hearts' content.

Theirs is a migratory flight not to compare with that of the songbirds which resort thousands of miles to Africa, but a migratory journey nonethe-less.

But not all waders depart to shores and estuaries. In recent weeks I have several times put up a woodcock from the side of our road.

Here is a shy woodland bird with which I have often communed during badger-watching expeditions.

Like the peesies, whaups and oyster-catchers, they win their meals by probing with a long, sensitised bill . . . not too easy when the ground is frozen as hard as concrete. In such conditions they have to search the woodland floor, turning over leaves to find rewards.

And in such conditions they also resort sometimes to patrolling the roadside verges.

It is the salting of the roads that brings them so close to man aboard his hurtling steeds, for the salt, in places, softens the ground thus enabling the woodcock to probe for food.

This too is one of the reasons why one sees so many rooks by the side of motorways. Such birds are not fools.

My disturbances of woodcock have all been at or after dusk but then woodcock are notoriously out and about at that time come summer or winter.

But whilst woodcock, and others, seem to have cottoned on to the fact that roadside verges can yield food, so far, at least in my experience, I have never yet seen snipe at the same game.

Yet they too have remained 'on station' throughout the cold spell, surviving presumably by plundering from the tussocky grass that characterises the kind of habitat they frequent, for beasties that live virtually on the surface.

They too bring a significance to spring. They usher the new season in by displaying and 'drumming' over their chosen territory. The curious noise made by the bird extending the two outer feathers on its tail and diving at such an angle as to cause the wind to vibrate them, is known as 'heather bleating'.

As the days of February are chalked off one by one, the time approaches when curlews will sail again over the moors, lapwing will advance inland in their tight little flocks, oyster-catchers will arrive in a frantic flurry of piping, staining their orange bills with good farmland mud; snipe will start their drumming, and woodcock their roding.

They will be joined by redshank from the seashore and, later in March by the sandpipers on their flight from Africa's shore. And spring will be here. Great expectations indeed!

Graceful beauty whose only predator is man

FOUR bobbing white posteriors disappeared, one by one, into the shelter of the trees as the family of roe quickly put ground between them and me.

So often this fleeting glimpse is all we have of what must surely be one of our most graceful animals. Roe deer are shy creatures, suspicious of man, and quite rightly so for we are, by and large, their only real predator.

A hundred years ago, such a sighting might have been a relative rarity for roe deer in the latter part of the nineteenth century, were not so common.

In some parts of the country they were distinctly rare. Now, thanks to a fairly universal policy of tree planting, roe deer are by no means rare.

Whilst the sight of a herd of red deer moving across an open hillside is stirring, for me at any rate, they do not match the roe for sheer grace of movement. Perhaps it is because they are harder to watch, living as they do in the cover of woodland, that they seem to offer a greater challenge and so rate as one of my most favourite animals.

I recently spent some time watching a buck with his doe. Both were in superb condition, their brindled winter coats sparkling in the early morning sunlight, sparkling too because their backs still bore evidence of the night's keen hoar frost.

The fact that they seemed unperturbed by this white rime on their backs was testament to the thickness of their coats.

A million strands of gossamer, also bearing the hallmark of Jack Frost, glistened and swayed with every eddy of the hardly detectable breeze. As they picked their way between the trees, casting long shadows along the weak rays of the sun, their breath was encapsulated by the atmosphere.

Roe deer are browsers — selective eaters. You will not find serried ranks of them advancing across a field like an army of chomping cattle. Instead they will pick here and there at choice morsels.

The buck had a particularly fine head, well grown but as yet covered in 'velvet', a living protective tissue which he will rub off in April as he begins to assert himself in his territory.

So impressed was I by his 'head' that I was immediately convinced that he was a master buck, well established in this woodland. It would take a fine fellow indeed to unseat him from his throne.

Each year roebuck cast their antlers in November and December, and immediately begin the business of growing a new set. This fellow was indeed well forward towards that new set.

On his neck were two delicate grey patches, his dark black eyes seemed to sparkle and his ears were constantly flicking and rotating to listen for any potential danger. Periodically he lifted his head to sift the hardly perceptible breeze.

His companion too was in superb winter condition. Her coat had a lustre about it which told me she had wintered well.

Slightly smaller than the buck, she too reminded me that her senses are as well honed.

It was easy to see also the curious white tuft on her white posterior, very much a distinguishing feature of the female, especially when only a brief glimpse of retreating deer may be snatched.

Unlike red deer, roe do not come together in large herds. Instead they retain a family bond. Small family parties are the order of the day and it is rare to see them grouped together in numbers exceeding half a dozen.

As I watched their peaceful passage through the woodland, I mused at how such a gentle looking beast can, come the rising sap, become an uncompromising and sometimes downright aggressive beast. As spring moves towards summer, when May fills the trees with leaf, he will stake out his territory anew in these woods.

Then his head will be clean and he will thrash the trees — usually saplings — with his new accoutrements, marking his territory visually and, more subtly with scent from glands on his forehead. Then he is ready to take on all comers. The gruff bark of the roebuck is, when territorial challenges are afoot, repeated and answered in a game of bluff and counter bluff.

Even now there will be a faint stirring in the doe. Although she mated as long ago as July, her twin youngsters are only now beginning to develop inside her. Roe deer alone of the hoofed animals use that remarkable technique of delayed implantation to ensure that when the young are born, in May or June, feeding conditions will be at their best to ensure a rich and ready supply of milk.

Perhaps, when winter's icy blast is past and summer days linger long, I shall again have the pleasure of sharing with this pair, a few more minutes of their lives and, hopefully, see them nurture the next generation of their kind.

Tit family

OF ALL the birds that flock to my bird table, and no doubt to bird tables all over Britain, none, I suspect, is more popular than the blue tit. It is perhaps the combination of blue, yellow and white plumage, so attractively distributed, their athleticism and generally perky demeanour that endears them so much to even the most casual bird watcher.

Almost as commonplace and, I imagine, almost as popular, is the larger and bolder great tit. And when I say bolder, I mean bolder. Few birds are as competitive and few birds are as prepared to get involved in a scrap in order to either defend a food source or a territory.

Less common, but just as attractive, is the coal tit. As perhaps the name implies, there is a comparative lack of brighter colours about the plumage of this, the smallest member of the tit-mouse family.

The most obvious physical feature of the wee coal tit is the white patch at the nape of the neck which bites into the coal black crown of the head.

These are the three kinds of tit most familiar to folk and apart from their relative similarity in size and appearance, they all make an impression upon us, I'm sure, because of their feverish energy and their willingness to live cheek by jowl with mankind . . . especially throughout the winter months when their main source of food, insects, is obviously much harder to find.

No doubt, humankind has played its part in the survival story of all three too. But of course, all three also show a well adapted lifestyle to help that survival story. They are, for instance, very omniverous in their diet, happy to forsake their insect diet for one of peanuts, bird seed, suet and a whole host of other goodies provided by the hand of man.

But they are also particularly prolific breeders, rolling off successive clutches of youngsters throughout the summer and always going for large families — often into double figures.

But of course such prolific breeding is an indicator in itself that this is a group of birds which is vulnerable. That is why they have to re-produce at a fast rate.

I often hear comments from readers about predation upon tits by sparrow-hawks which have also realised that the human habit of attracting birds to gardens by offerings of food, provides feeding opportunities for them too.

So it does sometimes shock people to have a sparrowhawk snatching the very bird they have been feeding, before their very eyes. But this is the way in which nature works. Cruel though it may seem, what they are witnessing is the constant battle for survival by tits and hawks alike.

And the fact is that nature constantly promotes the theme of the survival of the fittest. Thus any bird under par is bound to be the first target every time. That is not to say that perfectly fit birds do not also fall victim to the wiles of hawks. Of course they do. But the fittest always have a greater chance of survival.

The other member of the tit family possibly familiar to many of you is the one I regard as the most attractive of all, the long tailed tit. Perhaps this is rather less familiar in garden situations for they do not as readily visit bird tables. They are more often seen in little parties filtering through the trees and shrubbery in their ceaseless and energetic search for insect food. Perhaps they are also not quite as omniverous in their diet.

The flickering flight of groups of long tailed tits through such vegetation always accompanied by a constant, high pitched banter, is one of my favourite countryside sights.

They too are obvious targets for sparrowhawks and they too are prolific breeders. But, whereas the coaltits and bluetits seem to always nest in holes, hence their occupation of nest boxes, long tailed tits have a particularly well-developed nest building technique.

In fact, few nests can match the nest built by the long tailed tit, for quality and intricacy of construction.

The main building material is moss bound together with cobwebs and hair, with feathers for a lining. Bramble bushes and the like, which add to the defence system, are favoured sites.

It is quite amusing to watch a long tailed tit enter such a dome like nest, through a tiny aperture high up on one side, and wonder what on earth it can do with its long tail which is almost always much longer than the nest is wide. In fact, the tail is folded forward, over the bird's head in order to accommodate it.

One other member of the tit family is to be found regularly in Scotland but only in the north east, the crested tit.

Once, crested tits were widespread throughout Scotland but with the depletion of the natural forests of Scots pine, their numbers were severely reduced and they hung on in the far north east only.

Their population beyond this country takes them right across Europe and, with more planting, especially, thank goodness, of our native pines, they are beginning to extend their very limited range in Scotland.

In some ways, crested tits are typical of their clan, small, active, ever searching for food and in my experience, quite nonchalant about their relationship with man. I well recall one perching on the telescope through which I was peering at some other birds of a more famous reputation which are also linked with Speyside.

I have also spotted the odd willow tit in this neck of the woods, but like their look alike cousins, marsh tits, these are generally to be regarded as English residents. They do stray north and some breed in southern Scotland.

The fact that bluetits and great tits are among our commonest birds does not in any way detract from the delight I always derive from their antics. I guess that they may be described as the great entertainers of the avian world. I also guess that they probably provide those who are less able to get out and about, the elderly, the infirm, with endless hours of pleasure.

For that alone, they deserve our support. I'm sure I would be joined by many of you in nominating the titmice of this world as top of the bird pops.

B

Buzzards herald in the Spring

HOW quickly the weather can change. Less than two weeks ago the countryside was at its most savagely beautiful, encased in whiteness which had us all shivering and the birds especially, huddling in miserable groups, perhaps seeking solace in one another's company.

Within a week the tempo had changed almost completely. Now there was suddenly an atmosphere of gay abandon — as if spring was imminent — just round the corner.

Snatches of song sprung from the chaffinches which form the bulk of the marauding bands of finches, which have been a feature of the fields neighbouring my own few acres.

But if there was a single event which somehow threw the countryside into a new perspective, it was the sight of a pair of buzzards wheeling about the sky.

Here was the preliminary dance of the season; the first signs that the sap is beginning, slowly, to rise.

The morning was mild and sunny. The snowdrops hiding beneath the beech hedge seemed to have multiplied overnight. And high above, those two magnificent birds were performing — perhaps for the first time this year, first stanzas of their springtime ritual . . . soaring higher and higher in unison, just as two dancers might weave a pattern on an empty dancehall floor.

The springtime passion is re-enacted in a million different ways, but never is it more spectacular than when the performers are birds of prey.

Most predatory birds provide spectacle in one way or another just in their struggle for survival. The delicate hover of the kestrel has a less than delicate end, at least for the ultimate victim.

There is drama in the sinuous dart and snatch of a hunting sparrowhawk.

Who could fail to be excited at the sight of a peregrine falcon stooping in pursuit of prey on scimitar wings; or fail to be entranced by the moth-like flight, low over some heather moorland, of a hunting harrier?

And whose blood would not course faster in the veins at the sight of a hunting eagle drifting over a hill, accelerating to a frightening speed as it nears its quarry?

Perhaps the buzzard is thus regarded as somewhat mundane. It circles endlessly on thermals, or perches for hours on some lonely tree, waiting, waiting, who knows for what! Yet this bird too has its moments of glory as it sails on broad wings, sometimes to swoop in relatively dramatic fashion.

They rise higher and higher, one slightly higher than the other, until they are little more than specks in the wide blue yonder, and then descend, first slowly but with a quickening pace until they are virtually diving headlong. Down and down until at some invisible signal they both pull out of the dive and begin to soar again.

Sometimes these 'spirals' may contain several birds, each showing off its prowess.

For, make no mistake about it, the courtship flight of the buzzard is as much a display of prowess as the brilliantly coloured plumage of say, a cock pheasant is meant to prove irresistable to the plain female.

Exchange the gaudy colouring for flying prowess and you end up with the same raison d'etre — the need to impress the potential mate!

Golden eagles, more spectacular

perhaps because of their superior size, go through a similar ritual, sometimes even seeming to touch talons as they dive. However, the territory of eagles is long established.

Eagles pair for life and thus they may be seen patrolling the invisible boundaries of their territory at any time of the year.

As early as November they will indulge in nest patching and generally seem to make the choice as to which eyrie (usually a choice of two or even three previously used sites) they are going to use in the coming breeding season.

Thus, right through the winter they can be seen periodically flying in to a nest site with material to patch or add to the tumble of twigs, heather and turf from which they fashion their untidy 'home'.

But as spring begins to stake its claim, such activity will be stepped up and fresh 'green' material added.

It may seem hard to believe that already the thoughts of some of these birds are turning to breeding but a few spring-like days can quickly raise their spirits and begin the blood coursing through their veins. Eagles, in fact, are notoriously early nesters.

March will see many hen eagles already sitting tight on a couple of eggs. But they have a long wait — nearly six weeks before the first chick makes an appearance.

Thus, all is calculated to ensure that the food supply gradually grows as the demands of the eaglets increases. Hatching in mid to late April will coincide with the first flush of young mammals on the hillside.

Buzzards are not quite as quick off the mark but these early courtship flights are a prelude to the serious business of spring.

I expect the activity at our local rookery to step up by the day now. There too the serious business of nest patching — of making ready for the forthcoming season of procreation — will gradually gain momentum.

In all probability, in the next few weeks, the paths of the rooks and that of the buzzards will cross. There is no love lost between them even though one seldom poses any real threat to the other in practical terms.

Any buzzard coming within range of the rookery is likely to find a posse of rooks giving angry chase. There will be fine displays of real flying prowess then . . . all part of the quickening tempo of advancing spring.

We may have some winter weather to thole yet but all around are signs that spring is slowly advancing.

The unwelcome stoat

JUST as we have been watching the slow awakening of spring with carpets of snowdrops and, even now, daffodils beginning to unfurl, so too can we watch the ebbs and flows — the transition of plants, insects, birds and animals into their different and emerging lifestyles.

The ebbs and flows remind us constantly of the fickle nature of March.

Landscapes one day bathed in sunshine with frothy white clouds sailing serenely across a blue sky, were, in a matter of hours swept by enveloping sheets of fast moving clouds which, as they passed, left in their wake a white dusting of snow on the hillsides and even on the patterned fields of the lower ground.

On a benign day, without the vigorous showers, I enjoyed a fascinating encounter with a stoat which also bore clearly, the evidence of transition.

Half white, half brown, here was an animal in the very throes of exchanging its white winter ermine coat for new pale brown spring attire.

Of course, it is possible that this particular animal never really got in tune with his winter garb. Sometimes stoats do leave a foot in each camp, so to speak, never quite making it fully to ermine and thus remaining piebald for the winter.

Whatever this particular fellow's history, there could be no doubt about his intentions as I watched him . . . he was looking for food.

The gravelly ground of this patch is pockmarked by hundreds of rabbit holes. In and out of them he darted, his white 'half' — the lower parts of his body — the very antithesis of camouflage, flashing in the sunlight.

The black flag at the end of his tail, raised like a battle banner, was a salutory warning to any rabbits that happened to be in the neighbourhood, of impending doom — at least for any one particular rabbit whose scent might suddenly 'switch on' this chap's keen hunting instinct to 'full power'.

Once on the trail, little will deflect a hunting stoat. At this stage however, it seemed that no particular scent trail had yet been picked up.

He darted from burrow to burrow — sometimes entering one and emerging from another as he also explored the maze of underground inter-connecting tunnels.

His pace hardly seemed to slacken as he weaved his way in and out except when, every now and then, he paused to stand bolt upright, balancing on his hind quarters, looking this way and that, whilst all the time sifting the air for tell-tale traces of scent which might betray the whereabouts of the absentee rabbit tenants.

Having fully explored this deserted rabbit town, he hurried on his way with a series of sinuous movements which took him quickly into a small plantation of young spruce and larch.

Perhaps rabbit, after all, was not to be today's main course for the plantation, fenced against the eager mouths of rabbits, sheep and cattle, provides instead amongst its now rank grasses, a perfect habitat for voles.

So slender and tubular is a stoat's body, that it can squeeze through the narrowest of gaps. The fence therefore presented no obstacle to him and in a trice he was through, bounding through the tussocky grass and at the same time adjusting his mental processes to substitute vole for rabbit.

If he was halfway through his springtime moult — another follows to transform the dull brown to glorious russet — then as the snowflakes began their descent from the sky, the following day, he might have wished to reverse the process and return to his full winter whiteness in order to retain a degree of anonimity and a few more degrees of body heat.

Although I soon lost contact with him, I could imagine him continuing his headlong quest for a meal, darting from tussock to tussock, exploring every tiny hole, weaving his way along the dozens of grassy passageways that are the province of his blunt nosed prey.

There are those who would still, at the drop of a hat, despatch such a creature into oblivion.

Stoats and their cousin weasels, are tagged as vermin, still very much persona non grata on many a gamekeeper's beat.

That they sometimes tread unwarily into man's domain and take, for instance, game bird eggs and young, cannot be denied.

But equally, as slayers of rabbits, mice, rats and voles, all of which are well capable of swelling their numbers rapidly enough to be accused of reaching plague-like proportions, they also show another side of the coin.

Thus it may be asserted that they mostly do more good than harm. We are more balanced in our judgements these days, thank goodness. Gone, hopefully, is the view that predators of any kind are to be regarded as mortal enemies and thus ruthlessly exterminated.

Could it be that the remarkable and rapid growth of rabbit populations during the last century and the first half of this, may in part be attributed to the wholesale destruction of predators that accompanied the rise of the sporting estate, together with the swift improvement of farming techniques which thus improved the food supply for rabbits.

So, whilst keepers may distrust them farmers may delight in seeing that darting, slender beast for the help it gives in controlling rabbits.

Foresters too will delight in the presence of such efficient vole killers. Even though, those of us who are keen birdwatchers will be aware that stoats can be hard on nesting birds, they are a part of our natural fauna and as such have their place in the scheme of things.

Killers stoats may be, but they are also attractive, sometimes literally fascinating; sometimes even amusing animals.

They do say that to call a person a stoat or a weasel is to really insult them. I sometimes wonder if the insult is not the other way round. One thing for sure, I wish I was as slender.

Stoat . . . or Ermine?

The glories of a new Spring

Last weekend brought further confirmation of the advance of spring. And if confirmation was needed, there, on a little flotilla of rocks that are like punctuation marks at the end of a small islet, stood those real heralds of spring, a little gathering of oyster catchers . . . Ghillie Bride is back!

Their piping too was akin to punctuation marks . . . not yet the fulsome and exciting crescendo of shrill machine gun fire. That will come as temperatures keep stirring the sap.

And from heaven itself came the endless reel of songs as skylarks began the aerial territorial dances that set them apart from others. An excited gabbling issued forth across the loch to confirm that the mallards too are thinking thoughts of the season of passion.

In fact, the air itself seemed to have come alive as birds of all shapes and sizes hurried hither and thither, I knew not where or why. The sound of music added another dimension as the surrounding woods began to ring whilst the sun climbs ever higher in the sky.

It could be said that rooks are amongst the sweetest of our songsters. However, that is a judgment based upon my own perception of song. No doubt rooks think their song is sweet . . . even tuneful. That certainly must be true of the female who is being courted by a vocal male!

Even before the ice had become a sparkling porridge-like fringe to the loch, the rooks were beginning to gather around their high rise city. Nests vacated in the autumn are to be repaired, relationships renewed and territories — small though they are — set.

Of all the crows, rooks are the most colonial. Jackdaws too are gregarious in their living style, but if there is an example of avian urbanity, then surely it is provided by rooks. And although they nest cheek by jowl with one another — almost in semi detached nests — there is still territory to be established and defended. And there are still squabbles over uninvited visitations by neighbours. Trespassers will be pecked!

House repairing also brings its little arguments as theft of building materials is almost second nature to rooks. Whilst a pair is away seeking out suitable twigs with which to refurbish their own family home, it is easy for neighbours to filch prime building materials from unguarded neighbouring nests. But woe betide the thief if caught. There ensues a summary judgement and punishment. Each bird is very much king of its castle.

Much has been said and written about "rook parliaments". That there is a pecking order clearly established in rook societies, there can be no doubt. It is most easily discerned when rooks are communally feeding on the ground. Those at the top of the pecking order get first choice of the best feeding areas, the less important feed further out and those at the bottom of the order — the "peasantry" — remain on the fringe. The reported "parliaments", in which observers have witnessed a group of rooks standing in a circle dealing out punishment — indeed a death sentence — to a solitiary victim in the middle of the circle is not so much the dealing out of a sentence to a miscreant, as the eradication of a diseased or sick bird. It seems cruel, but it is just one way of keeping disease in check.

Such behaviour seems to be limited to rooks but there are other gatherings . . . of a very different kind, which also relate to members of the crow family.

Many people have watched gatherings of rooks at this time of the year, in which dozens of birds assemble in a field and proceed to bow and curtsey to one another. This is a courtship trysting in which young birds vie for mates . . . and old birds which have lost a partner, find new ones. Rooks pair permanently.

There are similar gatherings amongst magpies which, unlike rooks, are not colonial. These are called "magpie weddings" and such "parties" can contain literally dozens of birds.

Again these weddings represent a trysting place where young birds find partners and, as in rook society, widowed birds find new mates.

Such weddings seem to take place in set locations and if you've seen such happenings, should you return to the same place at the same time of year, you are likely to witness the same ceremony, almost year in, year out.

However, magpies, like jays and carrion crows, scorn the kind of gregarious lifestyle practised by jackdaws and rooks. Hoodie crows, unlike their cousin carrion crows, show much greater sociability.

All crows share one thing though . . . that they are fairly universally disliked by both man and beast.

It is common enough to see members of the crow family being mobbed by smaller birds. The liking of all crows for the eggs of other birds — and sometimes of their own kind — makes them pretty unpopular.

Man's dislike of them is sometimes similarly connected with egg stealing . . . especially those of game birds. But the crimes that really label crows . . . and especially hoodies, as criminals, is their obnoxious habit of attacking newly born lambs. It has to be said that in this connection, they commit some pretty dastardly deeds!

Hoodie crows, which largely reside in the Highlands, seem to be particularly nasty when it comes to such deeds and their bad reputation has, in large measure, been earned.

And yet the character and intelligence of all members of the crow family cannot be denied.

One other factor legislates against crows, ravens, rooks and jackdaws and that factor is their black coloration. Whilst the brilliantly coloured jay is often admired when it enters gardens and the magpie with its glossy, irridescent black and white plumage, is praised for its good looks, few people express the same degreee of admiration for the "black" birds.

Such attitudes date back thousands of years. To our ancient ancestors, they represented reincarnations of the Devil himself. And even amongst my friends I can record expressions of deep mistrust . . . not to say, dislike of them.

And yet, the acrobatic flight of especially crows, rooks and jackdaws and the clear expression manifested in their dashing flight displays at this time of the year, is as clear a message of spring as the piping of oyster catchers or the singing of larks.

And they are most certainly not ALL bad. Think for a minute of the tremendous benefit of flocks of rooks on farmers' fields. They do much to clear pests such as leatherjackets. So do crows and jackdaws.

In fact, they are very much in credit when it comes to identifying their value to man.

The busy preparations, the mass flighting of rooks and jackdaws especially in the evenings and their incredible displays of aerobatics are an accounting of the dying days of winter and full of promise for the blossoming of spring.

April
May
June

Ratty is not a rat at all

IT was one of those quiet mornings, hardly a breath of wind; the river idling by darkly and the sky grey and overcast.

Along the river bank, all was serenity as vigorous new spring songs echoed from nearby hedgerows and trees. Most of the song seemed to be of chaffinch origin but in the distance I could hear the repetitious but mellow notes of a thrush, answered, needless to say by an even more distant throstle offering.

Lapwings danced over the dark brown ridges of freshly ploughed fields and curlews meandered overhead probably looking for suitable ground in which to prod their long, curved beaks.

Suddenly just ahead of me there was a plop . . . quickly followed by another. Rings of ripples spread over the slow moving water and I could just make out two minuscule creatures, swimming rapidly under the bank before they quickly disappeared from view.

This encounter with a couple of "water rats" as perhaps Kenneth Grahame would have called them, was typical of past encounters . . . and no doubt, future ones!

It may be that the term, "water rat" is an unkind and undeserved tag for a mere vole, for voles must surely be generally regarded as amongst the gentler creatures of this world. However, words can mislead. If the word "rat" conjures up in many minds, shock and horror, then vole could perhaps be regarded as more benign.

Yet of all the members of the vole family, of which this country boasts three — save for the island sub species — the water vole probably exhibits more vigorous defence of its territory, against its own kind, than any of its not too distant vole cousins.

Curiously enough, it also is a much more ambitious eater, frequently forsaking the strict vegetarian diet of the field . . or short tailed variety and the more or less vegetarian diet of the bank vole.

Favoured delicacies include water snails, fish eggs and worms, although before any angling enthusiast grabs a cudgel and makes for the river bank to waylay a water vole or two, it has to be said that in essence they more regularly feed on grasses, reeds and the like.

However, it may be that water voles, because of their more catholic diet, are marginally less favoured as food by some predators. It is also a fact that they do not breed with perhaps the vigour and speed of the other two voles.

Whilst river bank walking is very likely to bring about encounters with water voles . . . if only through the audible "plop" of them taking to the safety of the water . . . the short tailed or field vole is much more likely to cross the path of visitors to the countryside. However, it is almost certain that in most cases, the human element in this contact, is totally unaware of the presence of voles.

I guess most of us who have spent happy days walking the hills, would record little in the way of vole spotting. Yet the very hills we have all tramped are swarming with them, at least in the summer time.

The fact is of course, that voles are somewhat more sensitive to our presence than we are to theirs.

The next time you walk the hills, try and find time to examine the vegetation through which you are walking, especially if you are in sheep country or young forest where there is still plenty of coarse ground vegetation.

I think most people would be surprised at the remarkable maze of tunnels which, on close inspection, reveal themselves. Some are subterranean — excavated tunnels with very obvious entrances — and others are merely tunnels through the grass linking tussock to tussock. Nesting in the heart of the tussocks, field voles are indeed prolific and in some years, their multiplication rate can cause their population to explode into almost plague proportions.

Six litters a year . . . and many may already be rearing their first batch of youngsters on the production line . . . is commonplace. And when you consider that a female field vole can begin breeding at the tender age of six weeks old, you begin to understand how plagues occur.

In lowland Britain, the bank vole may be more numerous than its short tailed compatriot. They much prefer the dense vegetation of hedgerows, and woodland. They are the blunt nosed, short tailed occupants of many a town and country garden and, needless to say, often fall victim therefore, to domestic cats.

In appearance, all voles are relatively similar and very distinctively different from their counterparts in the mouse world.

They all, for instance, have that same blunt nosed face as distinct from the much sharper features of most mice. They also have hairier and shorter tails than mice. The water vole is comfortably the heavy weight . . . sometimes almost the size of a brown rat, whilst the bank vole is distinguished by its redder coat.

They all have another common attribute — though I doubt if voles think it is an attribute — and that is their importance in the food chain.

The number of animals and birds for which the various species of vole are an essential and life giving source of food, is almost endless.

Probably the most familiar vole hunter is the hovering kestrel. Along our motorway embankments especially, colonised mostly by the field vole which finds the relatively undisturbed acres of unmolested grass a veritable paradise, kestrels have not been slow to "home in" on what is to them also, a ready made food source.

In woodland and along hedgerows, tawny owls spend much of their waking nights, seeking out the scampering voles which, with woodmice, must make up a substantial part of their diet.

Barn owls too will take their toll, especially again of the field vole, for their ideal hunting habitat is the rough grazing so favoured by the vole.

Perhaps because it is fractionally less

The umbiquitous Vole

vulnerable, the water vole breeds at a rather slower rate than other voles yet it may regularly figure on the diet sheet of herons. Pike will account for others and mink and, sometimes otters, will share in this waterside bounty.

Voles probably account for the bulk of the food of weasels and stoats, And, surprise, surprise, foxes frequently get in on the vole act too. In fact, in many areas, voles probably represent a major part of the diet of foxes.

Buzzards, harriers, badgers, wildcat and even adders all take their toll of the vole population and all rely upon it for a greater or lesser part of their main food source.

So next time you go through the woods . . . or by the riverside . . . or out on the hill, keep your eyes open, for you are in "vole kingdom" and the other wildlife riches you may also enjoy are often there simply because of the presence of the ubiquitous vole.

The enigma of the 'lonely heron'

LIKE snowflakes against an azure blue sky, the flurry of black and white wings were the very epitomy of the rising tide of activity that marks the advance of spring.

As I approached the loch shore, relays of oyster-catchers and peewits rose and swept over the restless blue water before settling again out of harms way.

Their excited banter added to the wildness of the scene, for truly wild is the frantic and shrill piping of sea-pies. Only slightly less so is the more tuneful rise and fall of the lapwings chorus. Each time a wave of them took to the air, the bright spring sun flashed in reflection from their brilliant white underparts.

Much less obvious visually but no less tuneful, a straggling flock of curlews joined this hurried flight.

The music thus made, backed by the everlasting song of larks and a multitude of other sweet songs brought forth by an uncommonly beautiful spring day, seemed to lift my spirit as I made for the tall pines on top of which I could see were perched a gaggle of herons.

Several of these strange, almost pre-historic birds, were also standing motionless in the shallows. Around them

paddled a few mallard, drakes now very attentive towards the plainer duck.

My approach sent the mallards scuttling low across the water and one by one the herons ceased to be motionless, opened their large wings and also departed.

As each one took to the wing, there issued the raucous cry that is so typical of this curious and somewhat enigmatic bird.

By no stretch of the imagination could it be said that the music of the heron is sweet.

Sweetness is not a description I would apply to the voice of the 'lonely heron' nor, come to think of it, to any other part of the heron's lifestyle.

But if such remarks insult the herons of this world, then let me redress the balance. They are, by any measure, fascinating and at times, graceful birds. Atop these magnificent Scots pines, there roosted at least a dozen birds, necks craning upwards like periscopes to watch, with those eagle eyes, my progress in their direction.

In due course, I stepped unwittingly across the boundary of their tolerance and one by one they all took to the wing, again shouting their raucous protest.

But as each of them sailed off down the wind, I was able to admire their lazy yet very effective flight. We may smile at the quaint attitude of a heron in flight, head brought back on that long curvaceous neck, legs trailing behind.

But our amusement should be tempered by the knowledge that few birds fly quite so well.

Herons never seem to be in much of a hurry, they amble across the sky, but believe me, when they want to be in a hurry, they can really move.

They have stamina too and frequently undertake quite long journeys just to find good sources of food. Their secret lies in the very large wing area relative to a surprisingly low body weight. Thus they have exeptional "lift".

Few birds were so highly prized by those aristocratic forebearers of ours whose favourite pastime was hawking than the heron. Here was a prey which would put to the test in every way, even the doughtiest peregrine.

To succeed in its business, whether wild or captive, a peregrine must 'stoop' at its prey from above. The powers of herons to gain height quickly clearly make the peregrine's job so much harder.

I watched as my posse of herons quickly gained height. They did so by sweeping along with the wind before turning to face it and drift back above the tree tops that are their high rise conurbation, a kind of vigilante force patrolling their own very special neighbourhood.

And having lived for some years, with a heronry on my back door, so to speak, I can tell you there are other comparisons with human urban communities.

Firstly, in the spring and early summer when the young have hatched, there is a constant garulous noise. Secondly, heronries are messy places.

Their nests are untidy heaps of sticks stuck usually high up in the trees and furthermore, they are also, by high summer, very smelly places indeed.

The contrast though is in other parts of the heron's lifestyle. Later that same day, I watched a couple of herons stalking the shallows of a small, isolated lochan.

There are times when a heron can appear as an almost miserable object. Sometimes when resting by the side of the water, neck 'folded' down, feathers fluffed out to retain body heat, generally stood on one leg, a heron can paint a picture of apathetic idleness.

Here was the other side of the coin as these two birds, all slenderness and sleekness, lifted first one leg then the other to walk the shallows, necks extended slightly forward, large yellow and black eyes scanning the clear water for the slightest movement which when spied produces a cocking action as the neck is drawn back before the rapier-like thrust which seems unerringly to win the fishing prize all day and every day.

There was another interesting contrast to draw. The birds I unintentionally disturbed from their high-rise flats already have laid their first eggs for herons are notoriously early nesters.

As I returned later in the afternoon, my day was completed by the arrival of wave after wave of geese coming into their evening roost on the greening fields close by.

Whilst the herons may have begun their breeding cycle, the pinkfeet have a long way to go before they begin theirs. They will, I expect, still be here when the first young herons of the season emerge from the eggs.

By then however, the geese will have strong impulses tugging them northwards to the home of pinkfeet in Iceland and beyond. Only when they reach that destination, will their cycle truly begin. Which makes me think that herons are also somewhat precocious.

No salvation for Devil birds

THEY are not ordinary citizens for they have played by the Indian Ocean, experienced the steamy heat of tropical rain forests and the arid sterility of the desert.

They have also scaled the heights of a dozen chains of mountains, battled against wind and tide . . . and yet they are quickly recognised residents of many of our towns and even cities; gregarious and preferring to spend their summers living cheek by jowl with man, relying on homo sapiens with his constructional technology for a place in which to perpetuate their kind. They are, it seems to a countryman, urbanely raucous.

The devil birds, their sleek black shapes zipping across skies of grey, blue and white, have unerringly made their way on a journey which has spanned continents and a host of physical obstacles, as they have done for countless centuries, to bring their screaming chorus echoing round the chimney pots and steeples. Summer — even this reluctant season — would be incomplete without them.

Swifts do not somehow seem to attract the admiration of mankind in the way that, for instance, swallows and martins have. Even the most ornithologically minded of our poets seem to have largely ignored them whereas the swallow has commanded close attention . . . and even adulation.

Could it be that the seemingly total blackness of swifts — even though they are in reality, brown — still touches deep and lingering superstitions which inevitably link the mind to Old Nick himself?

And could it be that those or us who have seen at close hand these ever restless birds, recognise in them, a reptilian connection to a much dimmer evolutionary past? Could it even be that we are suspicious of a bird that once grounded, cannot rise again?

Yet to anyone possessed of even a passing interest in nature, here is a bird which, above all, personifies the perfection of flight. Prior to their arrival here in mid May, it is a staggering fact that for probably nine months or more, the birds you watch hurtle between the chimney stacks on knife like wings, have never been still . . . never forsaken the sky for which they are so well equipped.

Only when they arrive here to breed will they finally alight in nooks and crannies to lay their eggs and eventually nurture their young with bulging beaks full of insect life gathered from their airy environment.

Even then, evolution has provided them with special advantages to assist them in their quest for survival. Their eggs, usually three in number, rather elongated and white, can cope with unusual variations in temperature.

Thus is the hen bird able to leave them for relatively long periods in order to forage for her own food. Equally are the young, when hatched, also able to withstand a range of temperatures which enables the hen to join with her mate in gathering food.

There is too a curious adaptation of the toes all four of which point forward, to enable swifts to literally claw their way up walls into their nests under the eaves.

Their arrival in the past few days has added a new dimension to our towns and villages — a dimension of sound and movement — an exciting and pulsating rival to the ribbons of cars and buses which thread their way in increasing numbers into our tourist traps. They mock the uniformity and regimentation in which our so called advanced technology has ensnared us.

They understand freedom in a way none of us will every understand. Yet they too have a discipline to follow, a discipline which forces them to follow those time honoured routes of thousands of miles.

They must leave the plains, forests and deserts of Africa and navigate their way northwards each and every summer to take advantage of the long northern days and maximise the food gathering potential thus increasing the survival potential of their youngsters.

They say that on an average day, a swift may fly five hundred miles in its never ending quest for food . . . which makes the efforts of our marathon runners look pretty puny doesn't it? Indeed, they are pretty extraordinary citizens!

Harbinger of spring

THE little mud hut of a nest perched on the top of a rafter in my goat shed, still stands deserted, a silent and empty testament to the non arrival of the swallows who built it several years ago.

So far the May skies have remained relatively vacant of both swallows and martins and I fear that time may be running out. Has there been some disaster on their mammoth journey north? Has the Sahara proved too big an obstacle for many of them? Only time will tell.

My hope is that many of our summer visitors are merely holding back, lingering somewhere in the south, waiting for an improvement in conditions before setting out on the last lap of their journey.

The persistence of frost at night and the generally bleak temperatures are certainly curtailing insect activity and that must have an impact on the movement of birds which rely upon insects for food — and that applies to most incoming migrants.

Spring is indeed this year a reluctant heroine but the past week has at least seen the arrival, in some numbers, of the traditional harbinger of spring.

When it was fashionable to write to "The Times" — an exercise limited to the south coast of England, by the very nature of things — small boys and not so small boys played an equally fashionable game, secreting themselves in suitable countryside and mimicking the cuckoo. How many "claims" such activity presaged is anyone's guess but the fact is that even in the south cuckoos do not generally arrive until April is a few days old. And here in the "frozen north", such arrivals are correspondingly later.

Young Cuckoo

Indeed, I do not usually encounter cuckoos until May Day is past. Cuckoos seem to be creatures of habit, less influenced by the whims of the weather than many other migrating birds. Their journey is generally shorter . . . from the Mediterranean . . . and thus they do not have that desert to cross.

It seems that cuckoos take the easy course in most sectors of life!

Undoubtedly it is the unique call of the bird which, over many centuries, has drawn so much attention. And it is, of course, a sound unsimilar to any other and thus easy to identify.

The resonant "cuck-oo" call is the "song" of the male. Less resonant and not so readily identified is the gurgle of the female which is in fact, marginally more musical and somewhat less obtrusive.

Physical identification has not proved

as easy. Down the centuries there has been constant confusion between the cuckoo and the sparrowhawk which even led, a couple of hundred years ago, to a widespread belief that cuckoos turned into sparrowhawks for the winter.

I suppose such an illusion could be created by the similarities apparent between the two species . . . at least at first glance. The long tail and generally heavily barred underparts of a cuckoo are similar to those of a hawk. Add to that the sudden arrival of cuckoos at a time when, in theory at least, the trees are bursting into leaf, makes it much more difficult to spot a skulking sparrowhawk, whereas in winter time the hawk is more readily seen.

Poets may wax in lyrical mood about the curious and sometimes comic cuckoo. I find little romance in its lifestyle. We may, in literature, welcome most avidly this "harbinger of spring". I doubt if meadow pipits, dunnocks, reed warblers and the 50 or so species of bird known to have been used as foster parents by cuckoos for their young, offer such a welcome.

In this part of the world, the meadow pipit is the most popular choice. The nesting density of meadow pipits in areas of tussocky grass, is surprisingly high. The sheep walks and generally unimproved grazings of the uplands will find them living almost cheek by jowl with one another.

Their nests are carefully concealed in tufts or tussocks of grass — so well concealed that they can be very difficult to find. However, the female cuckoo is a keen observer of the habits of meadow pipits.

The first thing a female cuckoo will do on her arrival here, is to stake out her territory. It is she, unusually, and not the male, who sets up territory. Having found a mate, her next task is to find just where the pipit nests are located. Most sightings of cuckoos seem to occur when they perch on overhead wires and in fact they make excellent observation posts from which to survey the surrounding countryside. Thus begins the market research.

The survey is conducted carefully and cunningly. She will make a mental note not only of the location of each potential nursery but also of the lifestyle of each pair of pipits in her survey. She will therefore be aware what the state of play with each pair is and when they are beginning their own cycle. Thus she will know just how to time her excursions to each nest in turn in order to lay one of her own eggs at such a time as to ensure that it will hatch either immediately before those of the host . . . or at about the same time.

Each time she visits a nest, she will wait until it is temporarily vacant of parent birds and each time she will remove one egg of the host before very quickly laying her own.

But from the moment of hatching, it is the bald and blind youngster which now takes on the role of killer.

One by one it will engineer all the remaining eggs out of the nest . . . and if any do succeed in hatching the youngsters will go precisely the same way. There is literally only room for one cuckoo in a nest and I have never known any other chicks to survive such an omnipresence.

Like Topsy, the cuckoo chick grows and grows until quickly outstripping what must by now be somewhat puzzled parents.

The final chapter in the story is that the youngsters will finally depart these shores at the end of summer, six weeks or so after their real parents — the cuckoos — have gone. Instinct, it seems, is a many faceted and particularly well honed characteristic of these unusual, welcomed yet unwelcomed curiosities.

Dawn to dusk owl

IN every sense of the word, what lay before me was a wild scene . . . more reminiscent of early March than a day or two from the beginning of May.

Periodically, the heather-clad moorland upon which I had ventured, was swept by rapidly moving snow and sleet showers, each shower at first obliterating the landscape before in the wake of its passage, painting it grey and, higher up, white.

In the intervening periods the scene was not even graced by the emergence of the sun. The sky remained a stubborn and depressing grey.

And to add to the wild nature of this chilly tapestry, down the cutting wind, there came the shrill cries of lapwing and curlew.

Indeed, the lapwings seemed almost to revel in the wind, contorting themselves into even more remarkable than normal flight patterns, rising and falling like flotsam on a high sea.

As yet another sleet shower brought a flurry of tiny capsules of the frozen north stinging into my face, I mused at the flashing white rumps of wheatears which darted away from almost under my feet in the heather. They have just completed a journey of thousands of miles from darkest Africa . . . for this.

A snipe perched disconsolately on a fence post allowing me to approach to within a matter of yards before zig zagging away into the gloom and a blackcock hurried down the frenzied wind, his cries muted by its force . . . 'go back, go back, go back'. That was probably the most sensible advice I could have had.

All this discomfort — or was I merely disgruntled? — seemed to melt as quickly as I hoped the snow would, as a new player stepped on to this hostile stage.

He appeared above a ridge to my right, impervious to the wind driven sleet. His flight path seemed to be heading directly for where I now stood, my back to the remnant of an old dyke, long since made redundant by neglect and the more modern fence.

Like a gigantic moth carried on broad wings which seemed to propel him effortlessly over the heather, he approached me at a height of about six feet.

His underparts seemed almost white as he flapped and glided but as every now and then he flopped sideways, he also revealed to me a beautifully barred and streaked topside to those long wings.

The blunt head of this approaching predator accentuated the moth-like appearance and also made identification easy. He was a short eared owl quartering his range, eyes down for an unwary vole.

If ever there was a bird which gives the impression of being as light as a feather, it is surely the short eared owl.

There is surely no mode of flight quite as buoyant save perhaps for that of a tern. But then those wings — the longest amongst our native owls — must represent a huge 'lift off' area relative to the total weight of the beast.

He continued to gracefully bob in my direction before landing, again as lightly as a feather, on a post some 10 yards away from where I stood quite motionless.

Now his heart shaped facial disc turned this way and that as he surveyed his territory. Two yellow eyes seemed to pierce the greyness. In fact few birds perhaps give such an impression of belligerence.

C

The combination of those yellow eyes and an appearance of lowered brows give an impression that this is not a bird with which one would wish to tangle.

However, in fact it is a bird with few enemies. Its main food comprises of voles and other small mammals although sometimes small birds do fall victim to its well honed hunting techniques.

When anything with a hooked beak was liable to fall victim to the gun or trap, short eared owls, along with many other predatory birds and animals, suffered badly at the hands of unthinking man, in spite of the fact that their presence on a moorland was surely beneficial and not, beyond the odd young grouse, of any detriment.

The appearance of the owl was not a surprise. In fact I seldom visit this hill without seeing one or more of them. That he had approached to a mere 10 yards or so was unusual but it gave me an ideal chance to study his beautiful plumage and return his baleful glare with a stare less malevolent in both appearance and intent.

Nonetheless he quickly took his leave of that post and floated down the wind to alight on another, his head girating rapidly and urgently as he searched with his eyes for the slightest trace of movement from the heather which might

Short Eared Owl

presage a light snack, if not a full meal.

Short ears are not an uncommon sight in upland Scotland and often colonise young conifer plantations which are soon alive with teeming populations of voles with other grazing animals excluded and grass thus growing wild.

But they have learned to be vagrant in character, moving on once the trees have begun to stretch and smother the ground cover. When I first came here a nearby hillside had been recently planted and short eared owls were almost as common as sparrows in a city street.

Now they have gone, moving on, tinker-like, to pastures new and food abundant.

It is at this time of the year, especially in the evenings, that the spectacular territorial flight of the short eared owl may be witnessed.

Instead of flying low over the moor, the bird now soars high, periodically stopping to hover before suddenly taking its wings below its body and banging or clapping them together whilst dropping like a stone.

This performance is repeated time and time again and there is an accompanying song, if it may be so called, a booming and weird sound well suited to wild open moorlands.

After post hopping along the fence, my short eared owl resumed the serious business of hunting, flapping and gliding over the heather before suddenly twisting and dropping with outstretched feet to pluck a victim from the heath. . . and life.

He rose again and took station on another more distant post, got out his serviette and cutlery and tucked in to a vole sandwich.

I suddenly realised that I too had become impervious to the stinging sleet. The visiting owl had me in such rapt attention that I had quite forgotten how foul it was.

When to leave little Bambi

THE summer's shyness, if not belied by temperatures and sunshine hours, is at least belied by the heady scent of wild hyacinths which now colour the woodland floor with a carpet of blue.

The lilacs too bloom, and their heavy perfume also permeates the air around my house. Such is the lure of these sweet smells borne on a warming wind, that the sounds of summer are also becoming evident with the droning of 1000 bumble bees.

Territories are now cemented. The larks spiral up and down their aerial and invisible corridors of power, each seeming to outdo its neighbour with the volume of song which proclaims to all other larks and to humans who care to partake of the joyous music, that this territory is taken!

Peewits are less buoyant just now, more concerned with the guardianship of their scuttling young than in proclaiming territorial boundaries.

Thus any gull or crow approaching is warded off with an attack so keen that retreat is almost the only course of wise action left.

New generations are emerging each and every day and many of our roe deer will, during these May and June weeks, drop their twin kids in secluded and secreted woodland glades.

Twins in roe are the norm . . . sometimes triplets . . . and each is carefully placed in some secret hiding place — each apart from the other. This is a kind of insurance against predators so that if one is lost, the other might stand a better chance of survival. Periodically the doe will visit each in turn to suckle and clean them, otherwise she either feeds herself or lies up during the day.

It is of course, in such circumstances, that people 'find' deer kids . . . even though they are inevitably not lost!

A few years ago, such a kid was found — thankfully a doe — and became part of our 'menagerie'. She is so imprinted on human kind that she still resides with us. Our weekly consumption of rich tea biscuits remains excessive!

It is of course tempting in the extreme to want to stroke such a 'Bambi'-like creature if one is stumbled across during a saunter through the woods, even to cuddle it. I doubt if any young creature quite matches the charm of a young roe, at least in appearance. I have said it countless times — don't . . . don't even touch it . . . admire it and then retire!

Scent is one of the vital bonds between a mother and its young. How else do ewes identify their own lambs in a milling flock? Thus to handle such a creature and taint it with your scent, is to interfere with that bond and even to run the risk of masking the natural scent . . . and thus the vital and sensitive relationship between parent and young. Such confusion can lead to desertion.

Thus, sometimes, we have to take a hand. But beware if your 'orphaned' roe is a buck. As we have learned with Zia, the roe doe, animals reared in captivity from a particularly young age, quickly lose their fear of humans. In so far as a doe is concerned, that presents few problems . . . except to avoid her sharp little feet on yours as she pushes for the biscuits! In the case of a buck, the situation is vastly different.

It is a fact that a tame roebuck is quite capable of 'gralloching' a human being. Loss of natural fear seems to give the fullest possible expression to an equally natural aggression which lies within most male animals. And with their lethal antlers at a particularly dangerous height, they can . . . and have done . . . some nasty damage to their erstwhile doting human keepers!

I have often used the expression, "gentle roe" and still maintain it to be a good description of the female. Bucks, however, are different.

A roebuck will defend its well defined territory against other bucks as resolutely as our country defended its freedom 40 years or so ago.

A few days ago, I listened to the vocal battle going on between two bucks in a nearby wood. Roe are not normally very vocal but a buck gives voice to what I would describe as a gruff bark as a proclamation of territorial sovereignty.

Thus a challenging buck will equally give voice. The result is a duet of barks and this is precisely what I was listening to.

Although they were out of sight — hidden in thick coniferous woodland — I

quickly got the message that the superior of the two was winning the battle and chasing, for all he was worth, his rival. Whether it was the intruder that was getting his just deserts or perhaps an older buck getting "What for" from a younger and fitter rival, I had no means of telling.

The outcome was inevitable; one of the two had to go! And indeed, the following morning, I witnessed, at a distance, the outcome as I watched what I presume was the defeated buck, depart that woodland and make its way hurriedly across a good mile of open country to the safety of another strip of woodland.

Roe do not generally favour open country, much preferring, even when venturing out of woodland, a short and easy route of retreat back to shelter, and so I could almost sense the feeling in this fleeing animal, of total insecurity as it crossed three open fields sown with cereals. It fairly bounded through each field, clearing fences with alacrity, hardly stopping, save to quickly sift the air for alien scents.

His arrival in those woods would, of course, give him no guarantee of peace ever after! There too, another buck will hold territory, so he will probably have to go through the same bitter battle all over again!

If, as I suspect, he was a buck past his best, he may well be destined to spend the rest of his life in relative isolation . . . until perhaps a bullet ends it all!!!

Such is the law of the countryside. The good management of deer requires that such animals are culled.

Nature's law ensures that only the fittest survive to carry on their line. It may sometimes seem harsh, even cruel, yet it is a means of ensuring that future generations prosper. It is also a fact that one of the main services that predators provide, is the weeding out of the weak. And man is a predator!

Roe Deer

Running from the word go

I MISS the lovely calling of lapwings at night. When the fields surrounding my cottage were used for stock grazing, the summer nights used to fairly buzz with their calling. The increase in arable crops in this airt has certainly reduced their numbers here and, whilst some pairs persist, the population has undoubtedly declined.

Other people have commented, this spring, that there seems to be a shortage of both lapwings and curlews in areas where they were both quite prevalent.

I have little doubt that the changing face of farming over the past few years has contributed much to their decline . . . at least locally.

But as soon as you begin to explore grazing ground, especially on the lower hills, as I did the other day, the picture changes quite markedly.

The grassland I went to explore was literally teeming with lapwing chicks. Everywhere I looked I could see their little scuttling figures as they sought out food, sometimes by prodding into the soft soil, especially when exploring little wet hollows, and sometimes picking the insects quite literally from the blades of grass.

Young lapwings . . . or if you prefer, peesies, peewits, peesweeps, teuchits, chewits and a whole host of other pseudonyms . . . are comic little creatures, beautifully camouflaged in their first few weeks by that mottled back and head yet easily identified by their leggy appearance and the characteristic black collar.

The field was absolutely moving with them whilst adult birds swooped overhead uttering that wispy cry or simply stood around as if on guard . . . which is precisely what many of them were.

Had I broken cover, no doubt I would have been immediately bombarded by the adult birds. Peewits are very active in the defence of their young and, like all such ground nesters, also have an ability to "freeze" their youngsters with a sharp alarm call so that the young immediately crouch absolutely still to avoid detection whilst the adults themselves set up a series of distracting displays.

Not only do they mob any alien intruder, be it human or otherwise, but they are also dab hands at deploying the broken wing trick, trailing a wing as if injured to draw the attention of any potential predator away from the youngsters which, needless to say remain absolutely still, thus merging with the landscape . . . until instructed to do otherwise.

Most of the youngsters I was watching were, by my estimation, between a week and two-weeks old.

The following day I also had the pleasure of watching some young curlews which dotted a low ground field together with a sprinkling of adults. Young whaups are gangling creatures — all leg and beak, although in the latter case, not yet fully developed so not displaying the spectacular long curve.

What both these particular observations illustrated well was the independence of these youngsters — both in the case of peewits and whaups —at such an early age.

In fact, within a matter of hours of hatching, ground nesters like these are mobile enough to be able to run at a fair speed considering their minuscule proportions.

Furthermore, they are self sufficient enough to feed themselves. I have actually seen a young peewit running along with part of the egg shell still attached to it.

On the other hand, it will be about five weeks before the young peewits are actually able to take to the air. In the case of whaups, they are not in the air until they are approaching seven weeks of age.

The contrast between these typical ground nesters and other birds which are reared in quite different circumstances can best be demonstrated by a further observation — this time of young blackbirds which are most certainly not independent, or anything like it, when first hatched.

Indeed, when they emerge from the egg, they are blind, featherless and quite helpless. However, they develop at a remarkable rate and are on the wing within a fortnight of hatching.

I suppose the real differences lie in the type of nesting habitat and, of course, in the lifestyle of the bird in question. It should also be said that blackbirds incubate for a mere two weeks whilst peewits, for instance, sit on their eggs for about four.

Ground nesting birds are of course more vulnerable than the likes of blackbirds which build their nests in much more protected and less vulnerable sites.

The ones I have been watching were renting part of the chimney of an old house; others, as many readers will undoubtedly know, choose such locations as garden sheds. More naturally perhaps, they choose fairly thick shrubbery or hedges in which to construct their nests.

In theory they are therefore less vulnerable to prowling predators although squirrels, weasels and jays and magpies are quite capable of totally destroying a nest full of young blackbirds.

And, just a week or so ago, I watched a newly fledged blackie, still trying to find its wings, snatched by a male sparrowhawk . . . doubtless as food for its own youngsters.

It should also be remembered that blackbirds often produce several clutches in a season. Two is commonplace; even three. On occasions it may run to four or even five for a particularly hard working pair.

Lapwings and curlews generally content themselves with one clutch per season although in the old days, when lapwing eggs were considered a delicacy — thank goodness, a thing of the past — it was common practice for people to take the first clutch . . . in the knowledge that the birds would inevitably lay another.

So nature ges forth and multiplies — one way or another.

A polecat waif and stray

WE MAY be thankful that our ancestors eradicated the wolf as a native of Scotland some 200 or so years ago. Not that there is any lasting proof that wolves were ever much of a threat to people. However, their presence did present something of a threat to livestock.

Their final elimination, curiously enough, coincided, more or less, with the large scale introduction of sheep to the Highlands of Scotland. The last wolf to dwell in Scotland may have still been padding around when those first poor folk were cruelly evicted from their houses and forced to join the trek to the new world.

But the wolf was not the last animal to be exterminated in Scotland. The polecat also disappeared . . . but much more recently. Its demise came as a direct result of the growth of sporting interests in Scotland which placed more importance upon the protection of game than on anything else in the countryside.

All predators were seen as a threat to game and were pretty mercilessly hunted down in a bloody campaign which almost saw the removal of wildcats and pine martens from our native fauna as well as the polecat. Ospreys also disappeared and there can be little doubt that the numbers of birds of prey were decimated, together with all other carnivores.

Polecats did survive as a British species, clinging on in parts of Wales, where there is still a resident population at large.

There are also now, it would seem, polecats back in Scotland. As I understand it, pure-bred polecats have been deliberately re-introduced to parts of our countryside.

But in addition there are, undoubtedly, a fair number of polecat ferrets living quite happily in the wild having gone missing on rabbiting escapades with their owners . . . or simply having escaped.

I am not certain in my own mind, that the introduction, or in this case, re-introduction of animals such as the polecat, is a good or bad idea.

From time to time, non-indigenous animals and birds have been introduced here, sometimes by accident and

39

sometimes by design. The most obvious introduction which springs to mind is that of the grey squirrel, a distinctly North American animal which was introduced to some of our parklands.

The original introductions were in the south but sooner or later — and, I suppose inevitably — they came here to Scotland as well.

I know plenty of people who curse the day they came. Equally, in fairness to the grey squirrel, there is little doubt that their presence in places such as Edinburgh's Princes Street Gardens, adds something to the enjoyment of the place for quite a number of people.

The grey squirrel, as we all know, has done very well, thank you very much,. since its introduction here! It may be surmised that the rapid colonisation has to a large degree, happened at the expense of our own native red. And, of course, there have been introductions, albeit accidental, such as the coypu to East Anglia and, on a much more universal scale, mink.

But grey squirrels, coypu and mink were never native to these shores. They have however, found conditions here very much to their liking and accordingly have prospered . . . much to the disgust of most country folk.

Mink escaping from fur farms have proved to be quite lethal predators, especially in relation to water fowl. On our local loch, mink may be the cause of quite substantial damage to populations of ducklings and young grebes for instance.

However, in the case of polecats, they can at least claim to have been a natural part of our countryside before man took a hand and eliminated them. And, even though most of the so called polecats now abroad in our countryside may not be deliberate introductions so much as escapees, and thus not, strictly speaking, pure polecats but polecat ferrets, does that really matter?

They are, in the main, close enough to being pure polecats as to make little difference. There was a natural niche for them and presumably the new generations of polecats or polecat ferrets, must presumably fill that same niche.

Whatever they are and whether or not they are pure, they will, for instance, play some part in controlling the growing rabbit populations. And there is a further irony in that, for let us not forget that the rabbit is not an indigenous native either. Man also introduced this ubiquitous creature, be it Norman man (some say it was the Romans) 1,000 years ago.

Polecats and their close relatives are, predictably, doughty hunters. All members of the weasel family are well honed predators. They hunt by scent, just as stoats and weasels do and once on the trail of a potential victim, they display the same resolution moving with not quite the speed and fluency of stoats but with as much determination.

A couple of weeks ago, I was brought a polecat kit which had been found beside the body of its mother — a victim of the most awesome predator of them all, the motor car.

Aged probably less than two weeks and with its eyes still tight shut, the little creature has displayed a strong will to live and initially demanded food . . . milk . . . at all hours of the day and night!

It has been weaned off night time feeds — thank goodness — and has graduated beyond milk to a diet which now includes cat food! Its eyes may be expected to open any day now as I guess it must be approaching four weeks of age. It has, like Topsy, grown and grown!

Although obviously born in the wild, this one will revert to a domestic life, partly because it will be imprinted on human kind. Whether a universal programme of re-introduction is folly or wisdom, however, I cannot be sure!

Contrasting way

Bluetits

ONE by one the brood of bluetits ejected themselves from the nest box positioned high in the birch tree in my garden.

I had been aware of the success of the brood because for days I had heard the rhythmic chanting of the youngsters from the inner recesses of the nest box and had also observed the constant trekking to and fro, of the parent birds, their beaks stuffed with insect goodies.

Nine little bluetits now have to meet the challenge of survival in the world outside. Not all of them will make it.

They face a whole host of hazards, sparrowhawks, stoats, known for their tree climbing exploits, prowling owls which are quite adept at picking small birds from their roosts, and not least, my own family of cats.

The success of this particular brood is not in itself remarkable. Up and down the country, in both town and country gardens, nest boxes will have been put to similar use. The productivity of bluetits is an oft witnessed event in the summer calendar.

Yet the nest box they have used has been in position for several years and this was the first time it had been used.

Initially the youngsters assembled together in the damson trees in the orchard. But by the following day they had spread out and some of them had taken up station in the spruces in the opposite corner of the garden.

Thereafter the frantic parent birds cut a tracery of fast-moving activity in all directions, fetching and carrying;

responding to the vocal demands for food made by their ever-hungry offspring.

The rhythmic phrasing of these young tits is one of the most obvious examples of communication between fledglings and parents.

The chanting actually stimulates the parent birds to re-double their food-carrying efforts and find even more aphids, grubs, caterpillars, spiders and the like to stuff into the expectant mouths now stationed, for security reasons, around the garden.

Someone once had the patience to count the number of journeys made in a day by a pair of tits to feed their family. It amounted to 900! That converts to one feed per minute for every daylight hour.

The other principal stimulus for the parents is the gaping mouths of their young. In almost all young birds the inside of the mouth is very brightly coloured — normally red or pink — and the target area is even more picked out by a colourful outline — normally in yellow.

The stimulating effect of this bright colouration is most evident in young cuckoos.

On our heather moorlands, meadow pipits are the commonest choice of the female cuckoo to act as foster parents for her young. The great, bright, gaping and quite cavernous gape of a young cuckoo is not only known to send the puzzled foster parents into frenzies of food gathering activity but is, incredibly, sometimes enough to lure other passing food-bearing parents down to discharge their wriggling cargoes of insects and caterpillars into that ever-open beak.

Thus, everywhere one looks in the countryside — not to mention in suburban gardens too — there is to be witnessed a frantic flurry of activity.

In the case of small birds, everything happens so quickly. Although totally bald, blind and helpless at hatching, in most cases, within a fortnight of emerging from the eggs, many youngsters are already flying!

Within a further week or two, they are self-sufficient and finding their own way in the world whilst their parents get on with the next clutch on the production line.

The production of large numbers is, of course, a way of ensuring the survival of the species.

In complete contrast, birds of prey stick at one brood a year. Nor do they produce the same numbers. In larger predators, clutch size is just two or three and in smaller birds of prey, such as sparrowhawks and kestrels, four, five and even six.

And there is never quite the same sense of urgency in the rearing process. Eagles may take three months to venture from the nest; buzzards six weeks and ospreys seven or eight. Even kestrels and sparrowhawks stay for a full month in what must by then be a pretty smelly eyrie.

I watched a pair of buzzards come off their eyrie on a cliff face the other day, an indication that they have hatched their annual clutch.

Once the youngsters take off from their lofty eyrie, there will follow a period of training — a honing of natural in-born hunting skills — which must by September, be good enough to ensure independent survival.

Meanwhile, the bluetit parents will tear about in a frenzy feeding their next clutch, swallows and martins will continue their production line and rear two, perhaps three clutches, although few, I guess, will reach the latter level this year. They were, after all, a little late in arriving.

Ahead lies the silent time when parent birds moult out their plumage and thus stop giving voice. But there will still persist a busy to-ing and fro-ing to produce this year's batch of youngsters.

July
August
September

Agile vacuum cleaners of the summer sky

AS far as I can recall, my first real wildlife experience concerned a nest of either swallows or house martins. I can remember being absolutely fascinated as the parent birds flashed in and out of their little nest in the porch of the cottage in which I had been resident for the summer.

To this day, I shall never know whether they were swallows or martins and I suppose it matters little. At the tender age of six, I was hardly well enough acquainted with the different species of birds to discern one from the other.

Yet their constant to-ing and fro-ing captivated me. I had never seen at such close quarters, birds so agile and delicate. I had never before been quite so close to a wild bird's nest and never before witnessed the greedy gape of youngsters ever ready to accept the offerings of their doting parents.

Perhaps because it was my first such encounter and perhaps because during the subsequent weeks of what I seem to recall was a long, hot summer — like all childhood summers — swallows and martins have ever since remained particular favourites of mine.

I also recall the morning upon which there were suddenly no swallows or martins. The wires upon which they had perched were suddenly empty; no longer could I stand and watch, open mouthed, captivated by their dramatic swooping as they snatched countless flies from the air. No longer was the air filled with their throaty chirping.

It took some time for the understanding to dawn that my birds had left to journey to Africa, and it took some persuasion on the part of the uncle whose cottage was temporarily my home, that they would, come the spring, return.

I doubt if a spring has since passed when I have not eagerly awaited the music of both swallows and martins.

During the past few days, I have had cause to become closely acquainted with such birds again. A week ago, a plaintive 'phone call relayed the emergency message that two martins

House Martins

had been found abandoned. It must be presumed that they had fallen out of their nest somewhere and, for their own safety, had been removed from the possible threat of cats or similar predators which would find two young martins a pleasant morning snack.

Whoever rescued them and in whatever circumstances, as usual I found myself playing nursemaid to two more orphaned fledglings.

When I first took them under my wing(!), they were just about fully feathered but still retained the characteristic tufts — almost like ears — on their heads. They are such delicate creatures, especially when so young, that to handle them and force food into them, is like handling priceless porcelain . . . or so it seems.

Flies are, of course, their staple diet and short of scraping off the carcasses of the flies that have perished in their millions on the front of my car, the only other appropriate source of food seemed to be maggots which, at this time of the year, are stocked by the "fishermen's emporiums"!

So, for the past week, at regular intervals and with the careful application of a pair of tweezers, my whole family have been engaged in the slightly morbid task of condemning dozens of maggots which I suppose might have otherwise have had an even worse fate, to death. In so doing, however, we have given at least a glimmer of hope for life to two house martins.

They have survived this somewhat unnatural diet and are now consuming vast quantities of grubs at every available opportunity. Furthermore, they have become increasingly vocal, demanding, as they would in the wild, further supplies at ever more frequent intervals.

The operation has become progressively easier as they now take most of the offerings without the need for us to actually prise open their delicate yet enormously wide beaks.

At first sight, the beaks of martins, especially fledglings, seem minute. But what may be lacking in forward projection is most certainly made up for laterally. And, of course, they are designed to scoop up flying insects with their wide open gapes as they hurtle and jink through the sky. In that respect, they resemble flying hoovers!

I wonder how much the population of house martins has increased with the spread of human habitations in Europe? They are by nature, cliff nesters, but the spread of man's influence has presented them with more and more nesting opportunities and buildings are now very obviously, their favourite habitats . . . hence their name!

The colonial nature of martins means that once a nest site is established, more and more nests are added each year. I'm also sure that the fact we have cleaned up our air — relatively speaking at least — has allowed the insect population to increase and thus provided for martins and swallows a bonanza of food.

Perhaps martins are not quite as exciting to watch as swallows. They lack the verve and dash of swallows whose aerial athleticism is somehow accentuated by their flowing forked tails. They also lack the colour of swallows and do not figure quite so prominently in folklore.

They do not, for instance, boast those orange face patches which gave swallows a reputation as fire bringers.

But with their white flashing rumps and almost navy blue plumage, they do decorate our summer skies gloriously. And even if, by comparison, they only take the 'silver' in athletic prowess, they are no slouches! But soon we will have to restore our waifs to the wild and so the search is on for a suitable nest and parent martins that can't count!

Keeping his lady waiting

SHE stands guard on the edge of her lofty eyrie, a jumble of assorted sticks marking this year's extension as another storey was added to those constructed in earlier summers. The jumble is not really a jumble at all, but a well-knitted, solid construction job which, if not necessarily tidy, is very functional.

Ospreys do not build their homes to win design awards. They build them to withstand the ravages of Scottish gales and as they add more and more shell each year, they also build them so that their offspring can shelter deep in the inner recess that develops.

Because this hen has at least one youngster, she is typically watchful, her eyes for ever scanning the surrounding pine forest for any potential threat. Ospreys like to be high in their residences so that they can survey the surrounding countryside. They always build a nest with a view!

That they are always alert and watchful — ever ready to defend their eyrie against any potential threats — is probably owed to the past deeds of man, the only real enemy, outside other usurping ospreys.

Yet ospreys do not like crows. Few birds do . . . and for good reason. Nor are ospreys at all enamoured with herons, an enmity I cannot fully understand, save that they may be competitors for fish, albeit that their fishing techniques and methods are so vastly different.

The appearance of a slow, flopping heron over the forest in reasonably close proximity to the eyrie, perhaps on its way to a nearby lochan, is likely to send both male and female osprey into something akin to fury. I have seen an osprey down a heron into the water on several occasions — not a profitable experience for herons which, though they feed largely on marine life, do so from the safety of the shoreline, or shallows.

Occasionally she preens but suddenly her alertness is accentuated as over the trees I spot her mate beating in from the direction of the lochan. He flies in like some wartime torpedo carrying aeroplane, a lusty fish slung underneath, grasped in those powerful talons, head, as always facing forward to ensure the best possible aerodynamics.

As he approaches she calls in that curiously high pitched voice and receives a vocal response from her food winning husband. Now he veers away and overflies the nest whilst she looks expectantly on, he seeming to show her what a capable fisherman he is.

But he repairs to a favoured perch in an old dead pine, from which, some months ago he was wrenching branches to fulfil his desire for home improvements.

First he satisfies his own appetite with a few healthy lumps of fish torn from his victim with that powerful beak.

The eyes of most predatory birds give an impression of smouldering anger and ferocity and if looks could kill he would by now be dead as he keeps her waiting. She glowers at him, impatient, not to be eating herself, but eager to get her beak at that fish to feed her hidden young.

He responds immediately by gliding over to the edge of the eyrie and depositing the fish at her feet. She quickly seizes it and moves it across to the opposite side of the eyrie before ripping off a good sized steak and presenting it to her offspring. For a moment I catch a glimpse of a still downy head reaching up eagerly for lunch. The process is repeated several times but I cannot properly tell if her offerings are made to a single chick or whether there may be more than one. She simply tears and dips!

Presently, feeding time is over and she stretches her long wings and flits the nest leaving her mate to baby sit. She circles, a couple of times visibly shaking the dust of the nest from her plumage, before disappearing over the trees.

I am close enough to observe that there is a thick cloud of flies buzzing around the eyrie and I conjure up in my mind the probability that up there, with a mess of fishy remains, things must be pretty smelly. It doesn't appear to bother the ospreys. The male preens as had his mate earlier, but remains as vigilant as she had been.

His sitting stint is short, however, for soon she drifts back into the eyrie, first circling the tree a few times before settling with her mate on the edge of those sticks. He has a desultory moment or two of house repairs, making some minute adjustment to the walls, preens again and then glides away to find perhaps a sweeter smelling perch a few yards away on a neighbouring pine.

Much later, having removed myself from my secret, midge ridden hiding place below a humming sycamore, I sit by the lochan which seems to be the favoured fishing haunt, full as it is, of fat brown trout. It is a sultry day and the midges are here too, attracting hordes of swooping swallows.

My vigil is lengthy — perhaps the fishing has been good enough to keep both parents and young well satisfied — but at long last I spy my osprey friend, probably the male again, swinging over the trees and making a beeline for the fish filled waters.

He rises high above the waters, checking on those powerful long wings, tail fanning to brake as he perhaps spots a movement of fish close to the water's surface.

He courses over the waters until again he stands on air, his wing beats quickening, peering down with those magnificent yellow eyes at every ripple. He has seen his quarry. He steps down a few feet, hangs again and then drops again. Step by step he stalks his watery prey until he descends in a dive which, as he nears the grey water, gets shallower and shallower.

His taloned feet swing down and then he hits the water with an almighty splash, feet first! For, it seems, endless seconds, he wallows as he secures his grip, before, with frantically beating wings he rises again.

Triumphant and phoenix-like he struggles free of the water clutching another prize in his lethal talons. At about 10 feet he shakes himself vigorously sending a spray of silver droplets splashing back to the water below.

He adjusts his feet on the back of the still flapping trout and then steers back on course for his eyrie.

Another meal for the next generation of what must be one of nature's most glorious creatures.

I have had a richly rewarding day . . . in spite of the midges!

Hunting Osprey

Busy time for parents

THERE is a gradual lulling of the sounds of summer as birds now find it not quite so important to declare their territorial boundaries. Most disputes over territory were settled some time ago although cock blackbirds and thrushes have, in many cases, resumed song whilst their mates start all over again incubating their next clutches.

Other birds are kept busy feeding their fast growing broods. It has been recorded, for instance, that a pair of great tits, brought to their brood in a single day, no fewer than 900 meals. . . one every daylight minute!

The fact is that tits notoriously go in for large families — sometimes into the teens — and further, that tits are very rapid developers requiring a mere fortnight to be on the wing. Thus their growth rate and their requirement for food is astonishing.

Many of the smaller birds follow this pattern; large clutches, a rapid turnover of clutches and a consequential need for the youngsters to become self-sufficient in as short a space of time as possible.

The contrast between this pattern and that followed by birds of prey is considerable. One clutch is quite enough for our predatory birds and in general their clutches are relatively small.

The incubation period also differs — a mere fortnight for many small birds whilst a month or longer is the norm for most predators.

Even then, there is frequently a long feeding period required before the offspring are capable of going it alone.

It did not surprise me therefore to find myself gazing skyward at the weekend to admire a pair of circling buzzards.

I watched them come off the cliff face where they nest and soar into a brilliant blue sky flecked with massive pillars of frothy white clouds. As they drifted across the blazing sun their plumage seemed to be fired with light.

I don't think they were going anywhere in particular, nor do I think they were particularly eager to hunt. But I am quite sure they will have a healthy brood of two, perhaps three youngsters, probably a week or two old.

With a healthy and numerous population of rabbits pockmarking the fields below their eyrie, there will be no shortage of food. Their chicks, much less than expecting a feed every few minutes, will, especially at this stage, require food only three or four times a day.

Thus, relieved of the need to sit tight on her eggs, the hen was simply joining her mate in some pleasant aerial exercise. And, whilst the survival technique of great tits and many other small birds is to produce offspring like peas in a pod, rows and rows of them, clutch after clutch, most large birds of prey produce relatively small single clutches of two or three.

But all birds of prey have devised a particular recipe for survival which sees a vast difference in size between the oldest and the youngest in a clutch. This 'staggering' of their young is, first of all, a result of a delay in the laying of their eggs.

Secondly it ensures that, except in the most adverse circumstances, at least the largest of the clutch will survive. In years of natural food shortage the youngest — the smallest — will fail . . . and often provide its fellow nestlings with a somewhat grisly means of survival!

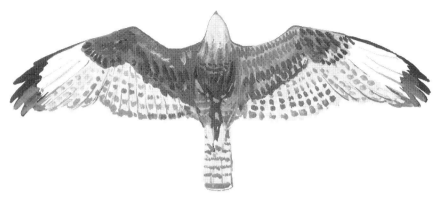

The Buzzard

So nature plays the percentage game — a game which, whatever the formula, is an almost certain guarantee of survival, at least for the fittest and strongest!

In most cases, the youngsters will have to find their own way in the world come the end of summer. The parents that nurtured them so carefully throughout the summer will expel them — sometimes most forcibly — from their territory as the leaves begin to turn.

The nurturing is a long process in birds such as eagles. Their young — and often only one clutch of two will survive — do not fly until they are about three months old. Buzzards cut that time to about seven weeks.

That hen buzzard would also be free to leave her youngsters for a while because this particular eyrie is south facing and, on the day of my excursion, warmed by the heat of the June sun and protected by the cliff from the chilly northerly wind.

Mind you, with the youngsters only recently hatched, the demand for food, though constant, will be satisfied by a couple of plump young rabbits, at least for a while.

Those two buzzards will, as their young grow, have to work progressively harder.

The same pattern is repeated in ospreys. One good fish will keep the newly hatched youngsters going for quite a while, even though the cock bird, who does most of the food fetching initially, will always take his fill of each catch before presenting it for the female to feed, first her young and then herself.

However, there will build up a sense of greater urgency — the female will have to contribute to the food fetching as her chicks grow — as the summer progresses. The urgency is accentuated by the knowledge that the young ospreys will have to be fit to undertake a journey to Africa in September. Some, in a bad fishing season, simply don't make it.

So whilst the smaller birds busy themselves rolling clutch after clutch off the production line, birds of prey take their time, concentrating on their one family of the year, and there will, I suspect, be less time available for the buzzard parents I watched, to cavort about the sky. There is a job to be done!

Red squirrel shows a strong homing instinct

A HUNDRED years ago, any sighting of a squirrel in these parts would have been of our native red. Nowadays, the vast majority of squirrels resident in the southern half of Scotland, are alien grey.

The introduction of the American grey squirrel just over 100 years ago to the fine parks of London, was quickly followed by further introductions, some of which, inevitably, saw the beginnings of populations of grey squirrels in the parks of Victorian Glasgow and Edinburgh.

So suitable, apparently, was the countryside of lowland Scotland that grey squirrels have since become one of the commonest of our mammals . . . with the possible exception of the ubiquitous rabbit . . . and probably the animal most often identified by casual visitors to the countryside. Ironic too, that the rabbit

Red Squirrel

was itself an introduction, if from a much earlier age, long before urban parks had been even dreamed about.

Here, at the southern fringe of the Highlands, the grey squirrel has certainly made its presence felt but there are, here and there, pockets of the original red stock. And, contrary to som popular opinions, some of these pockets seem to exist in spite of the presence of apparently healthy populations of greys in surrounding terrain.

The theory that greys actually attack and actively remove populations of native reds, has been long propounded. Yet somehow, the pockets seem to hang grimly on.

My own feeling is that grey squirrels, generally bigger and bolder than our much more shy red squirrels, are better competitors for food sources where ranges overlap.

I have never seen a grey squirrel launch an attack on a red. That doesn't deny the possibility of such happenings. In some respects, I acknowledge that grey squirrels seem generally to exhibit rather more in the way of aggression. I also acknowledge that, when handled, both grey and red are apt to bite . . . very hard.

Grey Squirrel

Thus when recently a cardboard box was handed to me, the contents of which, I was told, happened to be one red squirrel, my caution may be understood. The story accompanying the box indicated that the said occupant had been found in the forest in a somewhat dazed state. It transpired that it had been chased by a dog.

The "Jack in the Box" was far from being dazed. In fact, the minute I removed the lid it sprung instantly from captivity and made a beeline for the small belt of spruces in my garden, shinning up one of them at a remarkably rapid rate.

As this incident happened shortly before nightfall, I resolved to inspect the said trees early the next morning. I duly scanned the trees with the greatest of care but could find not one sign of the squirrel.

Several times during that day and the next I patrolled those trees but it seemed the creature had found them exceedingly unsatisfactory and had departed.

By amazing coincidence, I was recounting the story of the missing squirrel to friends later in the week, some three or more miles away, to be told that a red squirrel had turned up in the vicinity of their house — the first for several years.

Could it have been the same creature? By even greater coincidence

51

that house happens to be almost halfway to where the squirrel was found in the first instance.

It may be that I am adding two and two and making five. It may be that the two incidents are quite coincidental. But it may be that the same animal was indeed making a very determined attempt to return itself home. Whether such a strong "homing" instinct is present in squirrels or not, I cannot say.

But one instinct is most certainly making itself abundantly clear during these late summer days.

For whilst mankind, at least in this part of the country, is finding harvest time a frustrating experience, the squirrels of this world are most certainly harvesting very actively.

And in this respect, reds and greys behave identically. Now is the time to harvest surplus food and store it for the harder months ahead.

Both, it seems, have the strongest possible urge to collect and bury or hide much more food than they will need. This is when they work themselves into a frenzy to provide themselves with adequate insurance for the winter. Hazel nuts, beech mast, acorns and seeds are asiduously collected and stashed in little niches in the bark of trees or, more often, in scrapes in the ground, usually at the base of trees.

The absent mindedness of squirrels is legendary — a story based upon the apparent surplus of food, far in excess of requirements, that seems to be stored away. In fact it is interesting, during the winter, to explore such caches to see what other animals have chosen to share in the bounty, mice and voles especially.

The signs are easy to spot for whilst squirrels, with those very powerful front teeth, can crack a hazel nut cleanly in half, other rodents gnaw a small hole in the hard shell in getting to the kernel itself.

Much as the grey squirrel — the interloper — is universally unpopular amongst country folk, it is still to be admired, particularly at this time of year when it has moulted and now boasts its full winter coat.

Now it really is silvery in colour, save for the brownish tinge down the back. The tail notably is full and very silvery, compared with the duller hues of summer when the inexpert eye can readily confuse a brownish grey squirrel for our native red.

Country folk call these invaders "tree rats" — a rather unkind name perhaps. Yet on close inspection, and especially against the light, the tail does resemble that of a rat . . . with fur of course.

Without doubt the red squirrel is more attractive with its rich red fur and those lovely ear tufts. It is smaller and seems sometimes to move with rather more grace, at least amongst the trees.

There is another bounty for them, both red and grey, in the abundant presence of a wide variety of edible fungi.

The natural habitat for grey squirrels is hardwoods but they do penetrate our expanding conifer forests, if usually not too deeply. Our native Scots Pine seems to be the most favoured habitat for reds but the rapid growth of green coniferous forest in the Highlands has undoubtedly enabled the range of the red squirell to expand.

As yet the grey squirrel has not penetrated too far into the Highlands but its success and its adaptability is such that its range is constantly expanding.

That this is the most active time of the year for them and that visitors to the countryside may more frequently spot them is a tribute to their energy in building up food stores for the winter. But they too could find this a relatively lean year. As far as I can see, the hazels and beech have not yielded the usual crop. Still, they don't have bank managers to worry about.

Yellow yites break the silence of August

THIS is, in every sense, the time for the young ones. Just as countless human children are having their first taste of school this week, so too are many furred and feathered youngsters beginning to find their way in the world independently.

The field of rape next to my paddock, fast losing its yellow glow—and its sickly sweet smell—must have been absolutely alive with insect life the other evening.

Over it swept hundreds of swallows, feasting on the bonanza of flying food. These surely were vagrants for the general migration south has not really begun in earnest yet.

Judging by the relative shortness of their forked tails, most of this wandering flock were youngsters and I surmised that they would be the first born swallows of the year, now virtually abandoned by their parents whose attention has been diverted to subsequent broods of young.

So they wander around the countryside in company with a few non-breeding adults, probably drifting gradually southwards; going where the best feeding opportunities lie.

Some birds have, however, already headed south. Adult cuckoos departed weeks ago, confidently careless of the fate of their progeny the rearing of which they have left entirely to others such as meadow pipits.

The young cuckoos, now so large as to absolutely dwarf their surrogate parents, are still being pandered to. I recently watched a young cuckoo being fed by its pipit foster parents and they quite literally found it necessary to perch on its back in order to stuff a steady stream of insect life into that cavernous beak.

And suddenly the screaming of the devil birds which streak around the spires and chimney pots of our towns and villages like black darts, will diminish and vanish.

Swifts, unlike swallows and martins, content themselves with one brood of young. Once they are airborn, thoughts begin to turn to the journey south. By this third week in August they are moving.

Yet other birds remain amazingly active. The silence — the lack of birdsong — which sits heavily on August's countryside, is broken by the constant chantings of our local cock yellowhammer.

He perches close to the tiny cup of a nest in the hedgerow below, reeling away with his "little bit of bread and no cheese" ditty, proclaiming that his spouse is nurturing beneath her bosom yet another clutch of eggs which will be due to hatch any day now.

Unlike most small birds, yellowhammers do not moult during the month of August but delay that process until the autumn. Thus they squeeze in a third clutch of youngsters. They do indeed go forth and multiply! But so too do the swallows and martins. They delay their moult until they have completed their migratory journey to Africa.

But the yellowhammers do not journey so far. They are relatively sedantory, drifting south without the same purpose of the true migrators and moving far only in exceptionally cold winter weather.

The same pattern is followed by the skylarks which are also currently numerous in the fields around here. Like the swallows, they also wander about the countryside in small vagrant groups of adolescents whils their parents get on with the constant summer preoccupation of rearing the next brood on the production line.

All of these groups of relatively inexperienced adolescents are, of course, vulnerable to the activities of various predators. I watched a sparrowhawk drift menacingly along a hedgerow the other day, its objective to panic any avian residents which might be at roost within confines of the hedge. A quick flick of those broad wings and she would have been over the hedge and ready for action.

But then, I suppose that is precisely why some birds need to be so prolific in their annual breeding cycle. The young hawks are also learning their trade. Their inexperience is matched by the inexperience of the young birds upon which they prey, one factor balancing the other.

There are many other gauntlets for young birds to run. There are for instance, the wandering packs of stoats and weasels. these too are family parties learning the business of survival.

The kits are honing their hunting skills too, under the watchful tuition of their parents. They have plenty of practice on . . . young rabbits which are plentiful in the late summer and, of course, smaller mammals like voles whose prolifiacy is testament to their vulnerability.

But the young birds are also vulnerable, especially to weasels which are extremely good climbers. Indeed, within a matter of yards from where the hen yellowhammer sits motionless upon her third and final offering of eggs, I spotted some weasel footprints in the mud.

So far the makers of these deadly footprints do not seem to have detected the whereabouts of the nest but then it is likely that they are quite satisfied with the abundance of voles whose burrows pockmark the hedge bottom.

All these youngsters and many more are, in a sense, going to school, learning the art of survival, whether they are hunted or hunters. The lessons they begin to learn in the first summer of their lives are vital. If they do not learn them properly, they are unlikely to survive to see another summer.

I suppose you could almost say the same about those children whose first days at school these are . . . except of course to say that surival in human society is perhaps not quite so harsh! Although sometimes I wonder!

Yellowhammer

Hunters play a vital role

THE game of pool, which in recent years seems to have become so popular, is started by a player sending the cue ball into the pack of numbered balls in the hope that one or more of them might drop into a pocket. In that respect, there is a marked degree of chance about the game at its beginning, if not subsequently.

It may seem a curious analogy but the antics of a sparrowhawk I watched recently, seemed to exactly mirror that first break at pool when it suddenly launched itself at a substantial pack of starlings which were, at the time, perched in a black line along the electricity lines.

The starlings exploded in a total panic, birds scattering, it seemed to me, in every direction, accelerating outwards like a star burst. But the sparrowhawk on this occasion failed to secure his expected meal for not one starling obliged in presenting itself as a suitable target . . . just as, when I break off at pool, the balls fail to drop!

In general, all that most of us see of a sparrowhawk in action is simply that brief glimpse of a grey bird hurtling through space. It is usually gone in a matter of seconds.

Those readers who regularly feed birds in their garden, may have had the opportunity of slightly closer observations. Sparrowhawks are cute enough to have worked out that there are a lot of birds to be found in the vicinity of a well stocked bird-table, and thus a steady supply of meals to be won.

In fact, I know that there are plenty of people who take umbrage at the intrusion of a sparrowhawk and complain that the bird is taking the very birds they are setting out to feed. But this is all part and parcel of the food chain. Those small birds themselves, for instance, may, in the spring, eat the caterpillars of some of our most beautiful butterflies. And it is a fact that, generally, predation of this kind eliminates the weaker birds, even if we ourselves cannot see such weaknesses.

In this way, the stronger survive and thus the future stock of a species is itself strengthened.

In its hunting techniques, the sparrowhawk is covert. It often literally ambushes its victims, lurking in the branches of a tree perhaps on the edge of a woodland, along some forest ride or close to a clearing, from whence it can launch itself at a passing bird. Sometimes a hawk will also use the cunning device of speeding low along one side of a hedge to flush small birds, and then hopping over the hedge to take them as they flee.

In absolute contrast, the kestrel is by any standards, overt in its hunting habits. If there is one bird of prey most people have actually seen and witnessed going about its daily work, then surely that bird is the kestrel. Curiously enough, although many people are indeed familiar with the hovering kestrel, for some obscure reason, there remains a tendency for kestrels to be called sparrowhawks . . . I know not why!

The sight — the glorious sight, if you ask me — of a kestrel hovering on those trembling scimitar wings, tail fanning this way and that to make minute corrections to ensure that, in spite of sometimes strong winds, the head stays rock still, is a sight of which I never tire.

And, whilst they are no slouches, kestrals are no match for sparrowhawks when it comes to speed and manoeuverability. Yet they have, in some cases, clearly mastered a hawk-like technique!

In the more rural areas, another bird of prey which is relatively overt in its movements, is the buzzard, frequently seen circling lazily over a woodland or across open fields. Lazy it may appear but believe me those wonderfully sharp eyes will be searching ceaselessly for food opportunities. Buzzards may well turn their endeavours to a wide range of food sources, from worms to carrion.

They are opportunists but their ability to extend themselves in terms of hunting techniques should not be underestimated. You may remember my fairly recent description of a buzzard turning to sparrowhawk techniques and snatching a blackbird as it fled from a hedge, in mid air.

And I have often watched in awe as a buzzard has launched itself in a shallow dive at a rabbit. No, buzzards should not be underestimated!

I also had occasion recently to watch the stealthy hunting technique of a male hen harrier as it flopped its way across some fields, flying quite low and obviously at half throttle but ready to accelerate in a trice at the sight of potential prey — small birds or mammals.

Generally, the technique is to pounce on prey and strike with those lightning fast feet, bringing prey immediately to ground and there is a distinctive grace and buoyancy about the flight of a harrier, a grace perhaps accentuated in the male by that handsome grey and white plumage.

In the harrier's case, swift reflexes are the name of the game and I suppose the same might be said of the sparrowhawk although speed over a short distance and an agility enabling the hawk to zig zag through woodland are also essential.

But when it comes to speed — sheer speed — then one has to look to the higher places, to the haunts of the peregrine and the eagle.

The redoubtable peregrine is the real speedster. The hunting technique relies on sheer speed and strength. The falcon will drift about on up currents or perch on some suitably sited high rock, waiting for suitable prey to pass below and then it will launch itself in a shallow, accelerating dive.

It is a sight I have had the pleasure of witnessing on a number of occasions, and one which in my own experience, I have hardly known to fail. Various claims have been made as to the speed attained by a stooping peregrine — anything between 80 and 180 miles per hour! I cannot begin to guess at the speed reached by any falcon I have watched except to say it was fast!!

But then everything about the peregrine's appearance seems to give the impression of a bird designed with speed in mind. In the case of the eagle, however, because of its comparative bulk, we do not perhaps recognise that here, also, is a bird of great speed. Again, various claims have been made but it would take someone with a more scientific eye than mine to accurately estimate a stooping eagle's speed.

But again, speed and strength are the weaponry of an awesome bird of prey.

Each bird has developed its own particular techniques to ensure success and survival. Some are immediately recognisable; some more obvious, others less conspicuous. And, it seems, some we like and some we don't! Whether like or dislike is based upon the kind of prey taken by each species — and of course there are considerable overlaps — or whether our judgement is clouded by techniques we would alternatively describe as bold or cunning, I don't know. But I do know that each fills a necessary niche in the remarkable jigsaw that is nature.

The colours of September
-and brambles

THE chilly blast which accompanied the last few days of August, probably turned thoughts very rapidly to forthcoming attractions such as autumn! Indeed our hedgerows are beginning to assume the hues of that season already.

Bright red glow the rose hips; even brighter are the rowans which this year seem to be absolutely dripping from the boughs of the mountain ash. Do they presage a hard winter? If we are to believe the old tales from our folklore, then we are in for a big freeze.

However, I suspect that the copious quantities of berries are more likely to be a result of what is past rather than a portent of what is to come!

Having said that, I wouldn't cut down a rowan! Most of the older houses in rural Scotland have at least one rowan in their vicinity; their purpose to help ward off witches.

But rowans have a much more practical advantage to offer the birds. The rich and nutritious crop of berries gives them a really good start to the winter and although our own indigenous blackies and thrushes will plunder them, other raiders from the north will, before long, share in that plunder.

It won't be long before the fieldfares and redwings come rattling in like the Viking invaders they are. And when they descend on the rowans in their flocks, they can literally strip the berries from a tree in minutes.

The richness of the colours as summer begins to fade, seem sometimes to offer a kind of requiem for the passing season. The hills are purpled as the ling bursts into flower to join the bell heathers and cross leaved heaths which flower earlier.

Purple, too, dominates the hedgerows with ranks of fireweed — rosebay willow herb — tossing their tall heads in the wind. Soon that same wind will distribute their seeds even farther afield.

The thistles have already started to fade and it is knapweed — thistle-like except for its lack of sharp spines — which adds an even more brilliant hue of purple.

The faded thistles do, however, provide a bounty of food for the likes of goldfinches, those most lavishly coloured of all our finches. Bands or "charms" of these delightful birds are already wandering the countryside, feasting on the thistledown.

The bright yellow wingbars flash in the September sun and if you get close enough to them the brilliant scarlet face patches set them apart.

Their passage is generally also marked by a delightful "tinkling" chatter, a sound which it seems gave rise to the use of the word charm as a description of their flocks.

The mania of our Victorian ancestors, for collecting things, which resulted incidentally in the wholesale slaughter of both animals and birds in order that they might decorate the homes of the nouveau riche and which kept leagues of taxidermists in business, also bit deep into populations of goldfinches.

And, just as the depletion of great crested grebes for their feathers brought reaction in the formation of the Fur, Fin and Feather Folk, the forerunner of the RSPB, so too did the widespread trapping and caging of goldfinches stimulate strong reactions.

Fieldfare

The same Act of Parliament which sought to protect grebes also brought some protection, at least in legislative terms, to goldfinches.

I suppose too, the "tidying" of our countryside in more recent years, especially when so many of our hedgerows and road side verges were either eliminated altogether or almost sprayed out of existence with a selection of noxious weedkillers, destroyed many feeding opportunities for goldfinches . . . and indeed for butterflies too.

Nettles and thistles may seem an anathema to the frantic gardener but they are vital as food plants for many insects and birds.

The fact that sprays are not now used as widely — mainly because they are expensive and times have become that bit harder — means that thistles and nettles, along with a whole host of other plants, once again grace our roadsides and hedgerows. :

But there have been very few butterflies on view this year. Their late summer colour seems definitely to be missing and I can only presume that last year's exceptionally wet season hit them especially hard. It may be a few years before we see many small tortoise-shell butterflies decorating our gardens again.

And, if the fruits of the rowan are plentiful, then the same can be said for the brambles too. It seems that these late summer and autumn fruits are this year going to yield well. But then the bramble is a virile plant at the best of times, well able to cope with the vagaries of our seasons and adapted in such a way as to offer the maximum number of insects opportunities to help in the general cause of pollination.

Just now, the fruits are green but, given an extra degree or two of heat and a burst of late sunshine, during the next few weeks, there will be hosts of human plunderers to be found around our hedgerows.

The colours of September are glorious ... so too are those brambles!

Togetherness
- the winter ploy for starlings

FAMILIARITY undoubtedly breeds contempt, for if sometimes we are moved to rave about the sighting of rarer kinds of birds, all to often, we fail to admire the beauty of common or garden species . . . simply because they are so familiar.

I recently read that Russia's favourite bird is none other than the starling! Yes, the humble, much maligned starling! And few birds are more familiar to us here in Scotland, than that ubiquitous avian character, the presence of which is particularly obvious to regular visitors to our towns and cities.

In fact, the starling must be amongst the most successful birds on the planet. I watched and even photographed a family of starlings on a recent visit to the remote Hebridean island of Mingulay, which has not supported a human population since the earliest years of this century.

Equally, especially at this time of the year, wherever you choose to travel in town or country, there you will find starlings.

Just now the fast moving flocks of starlings are of relatively modest proportions. They dart here and there, living off the land by day, roosting, some of them at least, in the city centres, by night. They are gregarious and noisy; opportunists when it comes to food sources . . . and very beautiful.

Some may not, of course, agree with such a complimentary description. But take a close look at your neighbourhood starlings in bright sunlight and you will find yourself admiring the iridescent flashes of their plumage, not to mention the gloss and patterning of speckles which are their hallmarks.

Handsome they most certainly are . . . and quarrelsome! As they arrive hotfoot in your garden watch them also vie with one another for the food which has undoubtedly attracted them there in the first place.

Starling society seems always to be

restless and, perhaps like our human society, full of competition and aggression. And that aggressive trait is the main reason for their success.

The other reason for success will be more clearly seen in the weeks and months ahead. It is as autumn paints our landscapes with the richest of colours, that our native starling populations are swollen — mightily — by the invasion of countless millions of starlings from the east.

They come here to Britain in gargantuan flocks from as far afield as Russia, escaping from the advancing grip of winter which is, in the east, so much tighter than anything we experience here, even though we may be located on similar latitudes.

Here, on the western edge of Europe, we are blessed, believe it or not, with the balmy influence of the Gulf Stream. There are pickings to be exploited throughout the winter — except on those rare occasions when winter really does seize us in its icy grip.

It will be a week or two before the really big flocks begin to cross the North Sea and establish themselves here but already those starlings which we can regard as native to these isles are forming larger and larger flocks themselves. Their restless movement is beginning to pattern our September skies.

Starlings are not, of course, alone in flocking together for the common good. In the past few days I've watched lapwings moving about in tight little flocks, commuting to where the feeding opportunities are at their best.

It is also noticeable that the rooks and jackdaws are beginning to come together in quite substantial gatherings, although they appear by comparison to be somewhat disorderly flocks with no discernible shape or purpose.

Yet all flocks have a decided purpose.

Firstly, there is the huge advantage of numbers. If there is a profitable food resource to be exploited then the opportunity is maximised and all members of that particular group benefit alike.

Secondly, a large gathering of birds acts as a deterent to potential predators.

Starlings, although they seem as individuals and indeed as small groups, to have little or no discipline, are experts at maximising the advantages of the flock lifestyle.

With the possible exception of those amazing flocks of waders such as knot and dunlin which sweep our seashores, no flocks seem to display such a oneness and such a rigorous discipline as the large flocks of starlings which sweep like large black clouds throughout our countryside during autumn and the early part of winter.

In displaying such oneness in the air, starlings are thus, it seems to me, an anachronism. The collective movement of their flocks, each bird seeming to obey some apparently invisible signal from their leaders, contrasts completely with their quarrelsome adventures when they visit our gardens — especially when they home in on a bird-table.

Such concentrated and small food sources seem to encourage more and more bickering and more conflict.

The flock I watched the other day, emanating from an ancient ash tree which seems to be their temporary base, demonstrated perfectly this schizophrenic aspect of their nature.

As if in response to a signal they exploded from the tree as one, split into small family groups and proceeded to plunder the sheep filled fields for grubs and insects.

There was no acrimony and no argument. That followed when they returned to base and jostled for perches in the tree. Come to think of it, they are not that different from human beings are they?

Mad dash is on

WHEN all the world is, it seems, on a diet, the message for many of our native mammals is simply, "get fat"!

And whilst our own farmers are keeping the wheels of their gigantic combine harvesters well oiled, and at the same time keeping a very wary eye on the weather, nature's harvest is also beginning to be gathered.

The fact is that this is an absolutely critical time for both man and beast. For man, the success of the harvest is in some cases — especially after last year's disaster — the key to their economic survival.

For the beasts, survival is much more a naked truth; they will or will not survive the perils and vagaries of the coming winter. In other words they will or they will not live.

There is an urgency that has already seized those birds which have, or will soon, depart for the cushioning warmth of Africa. Their target was to literally double their weight in preparation for the mammoth journeys they have ahead of them.

The extra weight is their fuel for long overland or even sea journeys. If it runs out they simply "conk out" as would our own metalled steeds should they run out of petrol.

That same urgency will become increasingly manifest amongst the animals which, by the very nature of things, cannot migrate. They are anchored here, unable to remove themselves over the vast distances which flight makes possible for birds.

The methods used to top up the energy gap, provide a number of interesting contrasts. There are those which simply build up their own reserves of body fat and then travel in hope throughout the winter. Brock badger adopts such a course, feasting as the autumn harvest grows and laying on extra poundage . . . just in case food becomes short in the winter.

But throughout the winter, the badgers will continue their foraging in woods and fields, following old familiar tracks to old familiar sources of food and rejoicing in the discovery of any accidental or providential additional food.

It is quite wrong to think of badgers as hibernators. They will, if the weather turns excessively wild, sleep for a few days without even putting a snout out of the front door, but anyone who has lived near a badger sett will know that a covering of snow is no deterent at all. When the snow lies on the ground, you will find plenty of badger track to inspect.

Squirrels also gather food copiously but, whilst they may be reasonably weighty at this time of the year, their technique is to store surpluses gathered, not in the form of extra body fat but in little caches in the bark of trees, tree roots or in little scrapes in the ground. They are — both grey and red — notorious for storing far more than they need and for apparently forgetting where most of it has been hidden.

Wood mice and voles benefit considerably from these surplus larders of food and many a squirrel hoard ends up as a bounty for other small rodents.

Squirrels may also wrap themselves carefully up in their dreys during the really hard spells of weather and sleep for several days but, again, it is a familiar experience to have a "dod" of snow land on one's head as it is dislodged from the branches above by a scampering squirrel.

Most of the predatory animals — stoats and weasels for instance — survive the trials of winter simply because they are so well honed as hunters.

There is, it seems, always something out and about — voles, mice, rats or rabbits — to provide them with a meal. In fact, as autumn advances towards winter, stoats and weasels become increasingly noticeable because they tend generally to move closer to human habitation. They do so not because they enjoy our company but because the rodent population also moves closer to us to plunder our surplus food supplies.

For the same reason, foxes also become more visible. They know only too well that farmyards may sometimes provide excellent food sources in the form of rodents.

They also know that there are still farmyards inhabited by an odd chicken or two. But crafty fox has also moved closer to man for another reason. Suburban gardens and suburban dustbins offer further sources of winter food.

But there are those animals which do "cop out" of the winter by hibernating. The only true hibernators amongst our native animals are the bats and that curiosity amongst beasts, the hedgehog.

Hibernation also requires a good deal of preparation. That is why hedgehogs seem also to become less obscure and rather more obvious during the autumn months.

The key to their survival is to be able to find enough food to lay down substantial layers of body fat which, when they finally enter their "big sleep" will act in much the same way as the surplus body weight accumulated by migratory birds.

The difference, of course, lies in the rate of absorbtion of that vital energy. Whilst the migrating birds burn up their extra fat or fuel very quickly, hedgehogs and bats, by simply going to sleep and slowing down their metabolism to no more than "idling" burn it at an incredibly slow rate. However, hibernation is by no means a fail-safe method of ensuring that the particular animal will survive through the winter periodl

That hedgehogs have to have in reserve large quantities of body fat is vital. Especially this is the case when the winter is long — if it starts early and finishes late.

All of this means that animals are generally easier to observe during September and October. They are totally pre-occupied with food and thus seem to shed some of their natural shyness.

October
November
December

The climax of of the red deer year

THIS day began with everything satu-rated by the cloying mist. A thousand spiders' webs seemed to festoon the old yew, each decorated with row upon row of tiny dancing droplets of water.

Every branch of every tree seemed to be covered by countless drooping strands of silver thread. The cackling of geese marked the passage of unseen skeins as they travelled from their watery roost to scavenge in the stubble fields down the valley.

All that could be seen were a few tits swinging acrobatically from the nut dispensers strategically placed around my house.

It would take a while for the October sun to penetrate this grey layer so I headed for the hills.

In fact, the mist floated where once the sea had run for as I climbed the hill, I was soon greeted by the sun. Looking back, I seemed to be looking down upon the sea.

The whole valley below was en-veloped whereas here the foaming burn sparkled in the warm rays, the bracken glowed red and the sky was almost unbroken blue with only wisps of white cloud sailing serenely by.

As I left the valley behind, I could just make out the distant rumble of combines as yet another frantic day began for the farming fraternity.

The glen ahead was all that I could have expected from a late October day. Apart from the brightly - coloured bracken, the trees — mostly alder, birch and rowan, which chart the route of the burn and the smaller feeder burns that career down the hill — were mostly on the turn.

Many of them still cling to their greenness but the season cannot be resisted and several resembled what could only be described as nature's answer to the punk rockers, with swathes of yellow banding their very crowns.

Tiny yellow tormentils turned their open faces to the autumn sun, blue scabious nodded as I passed and there lingered still a few pink and purple heather bells.

A garrulous chatter marked the passage of a flock of maurauding fieldfares as they sped through the glen to rob the rowans of their last red berries, Goldfinches feasting on thistledown added their own very special blend of bright colour.

And as if I was suddenly transported by a magic carpet to the mystical Himalayas, a deep - throated drone lifted on the breeze, reminiscent of the chanting of Tibetan monks.

But this is no monastic drone. It is uttered by a stag intent on ensuring that he is not, at this season, to be celibate.

It is answered by another . . . and another. Ahead of me, high on a sloping west facing hillside, I pick out several groups of deer, the coats of the hinds even brighter than the bracken.

Each group is attended by at least one stag, none of which are so red. Their bulk is somehow accentuated by their darkness. They have, as tradition demands, been wallowing in the gory, peaty mud, a device presumably de-signed to give them a more daunting appearance . . . in a sense to give the illusion of even greater bulk.

The psychology of the rut is so important. Older and wiser stags, not necessarily masters, know that their success in capturing a reasonable number of hinds, lies as much in appearance and sheer brass-necked determination not to give way, as it does in actual physical strength.

The jousting is a war of nerves. A stag, already the possessor of a harem may find another approaching to enlarge his own. The approach is careful and the response also initially cautious. Each will face the other; each will roar a challenge. The wiser will try to attain higher ground to gain the advantage.

Such are the "lists" that are every year, the climax of the red deer year. I watched as the stags sought positions of advantage and watched as nerves crumbled and retreat became the order of the day. Only once did any physical contact occur as a stag approached just too closely to a superior beast and was put to flight by a sudden charge, suffering a rake to the rump in the process.

The hinds seem resigned to their places, showing little interest in the roars or the confrontations, alternately picking at the vegetation and looking on calmly.

I was not alone in watching this milling throng for suddenly from behind the crags high above me, a shot rang out; then another and another . . . a virtual fusillade echoed across the glen. I could neither see the stalkers nor did I see a beast drop. I had noticed a few stragglers on a higher slope close to where the ground dips into the saucer shaped corrie, much of which was now in shadow.

But doubtless some old stag, perhaps past his best, has seen his last rut. Perhaps more than one, judging by the number of shots.

These were the last lingering days of the season for stags. Now they will be unmolested by man for the stag season finished on Saturday last.

The massed ranks of deer now began to move — not hurriedly mark you. There seemed to be little sense of urgency although some of the outriders

did come trotting down the hill. It was almost as if they were unconscious of any danger.

Slowly they streamed across a burn and up onto another part of the hill, the hinds herded by their masters. Outlying stags moved with them doubtless seeing this as a possible opportunity to cut out a few hinds for themselves during the confusion.

And still the stags roared. Indeed, as the sun dipped lower and lower casting a chill shadow on much of the glen, their roars seemed more vigorous as if they were performing an anthem to the late afternoon.

The mist of morning had cleared as I descended by a loch now glassy, reflecting gloriously the hills above the opposite shore, basking in the afternoon sun.

A buzzard drifted by on wide wings, eyes down, scanning the patterned fields that sweep down to the loch for a bite of supper and a kestrel stepped buoyantly on the air, its eyes also seeking out any tell-tale movements below.

A gathering of mallard paddled about the edge of the loch sending out a succession of rings which soon dissipated on the still surface.

As I approached civilisation again, the air was full of the sound of mechanical giants gobbling up the grain and the straw.

Not a trace of the morning's mist lingered and now I could see the restless skeins of geese spearing their way through the still relatively cloudless sky as they sought the best and least disturbed feeding opportunities.

As darkness fell, the slow-moving lights across the valley marked the frantic endeavours of man. For some, it would be a very long day indeed.

And for the stags, every day is long too. Not until they have attended to their harems will they rest . . . day or night!

E

The struggle for survival begins

MY SKY was filled at the weekend by great, shapely skeins of geese newly arrived from their breeding grounds in the far north.

On an autumnal evening, their voices seemed to echo through the gathering mists as they departed their roost to plunder the fields of their unharvested grain.

These early arrivals are pinkfeet and in the main this is the type of geese we see through the winter in this part of Scotland.

As if to emphasise that this is the season of universal movement amongst huge populations of birds, as so many of them follow the sun southwards, the arrival of the first substantial flocks of geese also seemed to herald the departure of large numbers of summer visitors.

A week ago, I sat by the loch, its surface mirroring the hills, watching the white rumped house martins — and a goodly number of swallows — weave intricate patterns as they feasted on the millions of midges.

The casts of expanding rings on that still surface showed where martins were actually dipping to the water to pluck insect meals from the very surface itself. Theirs was the feast of the departing for almost as soon as the glimmer of an Indian summer descended upon us, they melted away and are now nearly all gone.

The midges remain, meals now for the darting night-time bats which must also feast in readiness for the great sleep. There is no packing of the bags for them, but a fattening for hibernation.

The ever changing pattern of the seasons has many parts, smaller patterns — cameos of life than change and mark, as they change, the passing of the seasons. The colours are fast ripening and soon the full requiem of autumn, in all its glory will fill our eyes with wonder as golds, ochres, russets and reds replace the greens.

Robins have resumed their soliloquy, wistful fragments of song which no longer stridently proclaims territorial sovereignty — even though territory remains close to cock robin's heart at all times. And new territories are being explored — kestrels appear where, in the past few months, I have seldom seen their hovering.

A young male kestrel had sought to carve out a territory over the fields and woods surrounding my cottage. I had seen him hovering watched him as he had taken up stations on the trees that line our hedgerows. These are brief encounters of the past few weeks which came to a head when, one morning last week, the loud protests of a kestrel came drifting across the wheat field.

Naturally enough, my curiosity got the better of me and my binoculars were soon scanning the trees from whence the protests echoed. At first all I could see was a bevy of crows . . . no doubt also imposing themselves on territory . . . hopping in agitated fashion, about the branches of a distant hawthorn. But soon the protesting kestrel exploded from the branches of the same tree — hotly pursued by the crows.

He flew directly and fast and soon had left all but one crow behind. But this particular crow — no slouch — was not giving up the chase. He closed on the kestrel, which, with a flick of those scimitar wings changed course. So did the crow. Several times he jinked and the chase continued for several hundred yards until shelter was found in a nearby wood. Only then did the crow give up and meander back to the same tree . . .

no doubt to tell his re-perched compatriots that he had given the kestrel 'what for'!

Now whilst the kestrel hardly represented direct competition, the fact is that those crows do not really relish the thought of a kestrel on their patch. Crows do have a particular aversion to birds of prey and they were, in trying to establish their favourite patch, making things difficult for the kestrel. I don't doubt that the kestrel will persevere. And I don't doubt that the crows themselves will be buzzed by other small and crow hating birds.

The Kestrel

A similar incident was witnessed when a mob of finches started to create a fuss in the kestrel's woodland refuge. In fact finches seemed suddenly to flock from all points of the compass to join in the rumpus. The object of their displeasure was a roosting tawny owl which withstood the verbal battering laconically with no more than a baleful look and an occasional clicking of the beak.

In due course the finches desisted and dispersed leaving the owl to continue his daylight snooze. The mice and voles hereabouts will get little peace with those two around.

Nor will we it seems! Each night, the misty air carries with it the monotonous hooting of, presumably the same owl. There is a response, in fact there are several responses from our bevy of hospitalised owls. They also hoot their reply and periodically, screech.

And of course, this too is a sound of autumn for it is now that tawnies set up their territories and now that they proclaim those territories vocally.

Whilst the autumn brings with it a final flourish of luxuriant colour, it also brings some duller hues. I stopped to watch a roe doe gouging at a neighbour's neeps the other evening. Her coat was the coat of winter. Gone is the bright red of summer, in its place the dark, brindled carpet-like coat of winter. As I moved away, my curiosity and admiration satisfied, her ears came up and she departed with a series of lovely bounds, her final spring taking her delightfully over the fence and into the thick wood where she no doubt spends most of her life.

And if further evidence of nature's constantly changing tapestry were needed, then that evidence is provided by the heavy dews of autumn which highlight the never ceasing work of countless spiders.

Each morning there is a new tapestry bedecked with thousands of trembling beads of moisture — like so many diamonds strung on some priceless necklace.

The old yew is festooned, the grasses and shrubs. Everywhere it seems, new traps are being set to ensnare every kind of insect. The net trembles as yet another careless fly is caught and, quick as a flash, the spider, sensing the impact, darts along the silvery strands to snatch her prey.

As October appears on our calendars, it may seem like an end — in the case of this summer, perhaps a blessed relief — but it is also very much a beginning as this year's new life begins the age old struggle for survival.

Telepathy in the air

THE continuing mildness of the season is certainly reflected in the constant tapestry of movement in the skies. Flocks of birds of all kinds, seem to be ever on the move . . . at least in my neck of the woods.

There is, seemingly, still a good deal of mopping up to be done, the last of last summer's rich crop of berries to gobble, rose hips upon which to gorge and remnants of the heavy harvest of cereals to be won from the fields.

In fact, the long spell of unending autumnal weather with hardly a hint of keen frosts, has unquestionably made this a remarkable bird-watching time.

There seems recently to have been a good deal written and said about phenomena like extra sensory perception. Well, I am quite convinced that birds somehow have a sixth sense which enables them to retain sometimes amazingly tight flock formations.

Perhaps it is an instinct or a built-in discipline . . . or even a well-honed reflex that enables such large numbers of birds to seemingly act as one. I remain convinced that there has to be more to it than that.

It is not so evident amongst loose and comparitively undisciplined flocks such as redwings and fieldfares, those loud, chattering invaders from the north. Nor is it so evident in the untidy roaming bands of finches that scour the fields for spilt grain.

But watch a flock of starlings . . . or a flight of duck and you cannot help but feel there is some sort of tele-communication between each flock member.

They whirl and dart in such unison . . . and in such tight formation that it would seem impossible for them to avoid some sort of collision' yet there never seems to

be any evidence of even contact. And they perform their various aerobatics at an apparently breakneck speed which makes their flock discipline seem even more difficult to account for, at least in normal terms.

A similar demonstration of activity in unison came from a walk through the mud to a small lochan which at this time of the year is always occupied by a few wildfowl.

As has often before been the case, I put some teal up and again I mused on the fact that they all seemed to leave the water at once — an explosion of frantic activity but completely co-ordinated just as was their subsequent and hurried flight round the lochan until I finally departed.

Of course, different species have evolved different codes for self preservation. No doubt the instant explosion into flight of those duck was also partly due to a vocal signal from a sentry. Yet the response was universally instant.

I also passed a busy rabbit warren on my way to the lochan and was able to observe the signalling system of the many occupants. Their signalling system begins with warning thumpings from one of the bucks and continues with the obvious bobbing of white scuts which is a clear visual warning to other inhabitants.

Yet never is the reaction to either signal as instant as the reaction of birds.

Roe deer also have a similar white warning system which acts not only as an alarm but also as an insurance that members of the same group can more easily remain together.

That togetherness is also a part of the survival kit.

Separation can often mean disaster - which is well demonstrated by the fact that predators often work on the basis of cutting an individual flock or group member out of the protective group before finally nailing it.

On the other hand, predators seldom work as anything other than individuals. I've been told on several occasions that foxes will sometimes hunt in packs.

Other than a vixen taking her youngsters on training missions and clearly demonstrating to them the techniques they must learn to survive, I have no first hand experience of the pack approach which is, in any case, uncharacteristic of the fox which generally is a loner.

In much the same way packs of stoats or weasels may sometimes operate in concert. These I have seen and again are, more often than not, family groups.

As far as winged predators are concerned, in some cases at least - and one thinks especially of sparrowhawks and peregrines - joint attacks on, say, a flock of starlings would presumably only add to the confusion that can sometimes be the best defence.

Only when young are being trained in the art of hunting can I say I've witnessed "joint ventures".

But what means of communication there can be amongst members of large flocks of birds can only be by vocal signal or reactive.

Thus can one witness those amazing tumbling displays of flocks of rooks or jackdaws. One sets the sequence in motion and the rest of the flock follows suit in a chain reaction which is as clear an expression of joy as one is likely to see.

It is, I suppose, a demonstration of 'follow my leader' syndrome. And that, perhaps, is the nub of it.

Whether, in the case of those enormous flocks of starlings the signal to move this way or that is at the behest of a flock leader and then purely reactive on the part of the rest of the flock, is difficult to assess.

It would be hard to believe, however, that there is not also another element - another sense - in operation. How else could such perfect togetherness be achieved?

The unpredictability of nature

ONE of the most predictable things about nature . . . is that it is unpredictable! And so often it is the unusual that catches the eye. Last week, I did a perfect double take when I spotted a bird in my garden which I could not at first recognise.

In fact my first view of the bird in question did not provoke much interest. It was, as far as I could see — and I had a rear view — a dunnock, one of nature's shrinking violets, an unobtrusive if not quite skulking bird, plain to look at but owner of a sweet voice. Even in the area of music, however, it never seems quite to fulfil its promise.

It was when the bird turned to face me that the neck stretching began for this particular dunnock was the proud possessor of a lovely white breast.

Shadows of doubt began to flit across my mind. Was it a dunnock after all? Immediately, I began to run through my mind other possibilities. It is at times like this that I recognise the value of computers!

But dunnock it was. From time to time, nature does come up with oddities of this kind. In fact, it was an exceptionally attractive dunnock — I would even go so far as to say that if dunnocks were ever to be re-designed, this would make a fine new model!

Birds with white patches like my dunnock are, of course, not new. Although it may seem anachronistic to say so, the most often observed bird with such white patches, must be your common or garden blackbird!

And, of course, it is not at all unusual to see a completely white blackbird which is even more of an anachronism.

A few years ago, I frequently watched a white starling which stood out like a proverbial sore thumb amongst its whirling flock of black compatriots. Significantly, it was always situated in the centre of the flock . . . never at the periphery.

This was, of course, a perfect example of albinism, a bird which lacks the colour genes in its make-up.

And a couple of winters ago, I also had a number of telephone calls from residents in Stirling who claimed that they had a snow bunting around their gardens. The fact is that snow buntings don't turn up in town gardens. Eventually, I tracked down the mystery bird and concluded that it was a white greenfinch — another anachronism!

Snow buntings may be seen in Scotland, mostly in the winter and mostly at either high altitudes or along our coasts where they feed on the seeds of hill grasses and dune grass. I used to watch them regularly on the Clyde coast and have had the pleasure of observing them on our mountains too.

A few pairs have actually been recorded here as breeders. But for the most part they breed in Arctic regions, right across the roof of the world in Greenland, Lapland, Iceland and Arctic Russia.

And it is at this time of the year, of course, that Britain plays host to many birds from the Arctic, some of them regular visitors to these shores, like the geese; others much more irregular and some, positively rare.

Sometimes, those rarities send ornithologists into an absolute frenzy of excitement. There has been excitement recently at the arrival, in this part of Scotland, of barred crossbills, another mini Russian invader.

Many of these unusual visitors have arrived here because they have taken quite the wrong migratory route . . . or in some cases, have been literally blown off course by inclement weather.

Birds like the Arctic warbler, which breeds again on the roof of the world from North America in the west to Siberia in the east, should be on course for south east Asia. The barred crossbills ought to be aiming for the Baltic.

One of the commonest vagrants in these parts is probably the snow goose, which, like our pinkfeet, breeds also in the far north but which, in theory, should winter in America.

Almost every year, amongst the flocks of pinkfeet, currently scavenging amongst the remnants of the harvest, an odd snow goose or two may be spotted . . . having presumably turned left instead of right and having travelled with the pinkfeet instead of with flocks of snow geese!

Some of the incomers are unrecognisable as migrants. For instance, it is a fact that many Scandinavian kestrels winter here. Perhaps the pair that have taken on the fields around me as their hunting territory are two such visitors?

Rough-legged buzzards also arrive in Scotland from the same quarter. They may be distinguished from our resident common buzzards by much lighter underparts, a light coloured tail with a prominent black band at its tip and, as the name might imply, by the pantalooned appearance of the well-feathered legs.

Periodically, really rare and quite spectacular vagrants occur. Most notable are the arrivals such as king eiders, colourful ducks which again come here from the far north, and birds of prey such as the lovely gyr falcon — usually in the form of the white Greenland based variation . . . and, of course, the now famous snowy owl.

In the latter case, much excitement was generated some years ago when snowy owls actually bred first in Shetland and then in the north of Scotland.

Amongst the most commonly seen of our unusual winter visitors, are the waxwings. Their presence here is very varied and like the Scandinavian crossbills, in some years, they seem to 'explode'.

Here is a truly beautiful bird, colourful and unusual which graces not the remoter parts of the countryside but which arrives very obviously in the very heart of town.

About the size of starlings but plumper, waxwings are lovely pink and chestnut coloured birds, possessed of handsome head crests. The males add a brilliant flash of yellow in the wings and at the tip of the tail both female and male sport another yellow flash.

But the feature that distinguishes them . . . and gives them their name . . . is the lovely wax-like red tipped flight feathers.

They are attracted to urban areas by the presence of berry bearing trees and shrubs in our gardens and parks. Cotoneaster and pyracantha are the special favourites and, of course, these are two species frequently grown in towns.

So look out for them, even in the town centre, for Stirling seems to be graced by a waxwing invasion most years.

Nature's winter tapestry

AS EACH day of the current cold snap goes by, the number of small birds taking advantage of my offerings of nuts and seed, seems to swell. I'm sure many readers are sharing the same experience and enjoying the antics of a whole host of garden visitors.

Suburban gardens, with their rich variety of shrubs and trees, provide shelter for a remarkable range of birds. They also provide cover for lurking cats! But in the countryside — or at least in parts of the countryside — too much natural cover has been eliminated as hedgerows and those wee wild corners have steadily disappeared as man has sought to extract more and more from his few acres.

I am fortunate in that most of the hedgerows here have remained. They are augmented by clusters of birch, rowan and hawthorn which fringe the dense conifer plantations, and between them they too provide marvellous shelter for a whole host of small birds.

A late afternoon meander along some of my local hedgerows perfectly illustrated their value last weekend for, as I wandered slowly through the neighbouring fields, my progress was charted by hundreds of mini evacuations of flocks of finches and tits.

There is still quite a harvest to be gathered from the hawthorns. A bevy of blackbirds was hard at work popping the red haws, one by one, down ever receptive throats. They scolded me and hurried off a few yards as I disturbed them.

One particular cock bird, in prime condition, his black plumage fairly shining in the brittle November sunshine, yellow bill almost luminous and those yellow eye rings seeming to enlarge his dark, glinting eyes, hurried to and fro with a real volley of blackbird swear words.

Mixed flocks of chaffinches and greenfinches similarly bounced away in that buoyant flight, the pink breasts of the cock chaffies and the yellow flashes on the wings of the greeneys catching the rays of the sun.

There were great tits, blue tits and coal tits filtering through the branches in their frantic search for insects and spiders . . . and no cats!

But there was a menace. As I stood in the corner of a field, lighting up another pipeful, a slate grey shape suddenly slid from the hawthorn ahead of me and sped low and straight along the hedge side, about two feet above the stubble. A cock sparrowhawk was on the war path.

He sped along for about 15 or 20 yards before suddenly lifting over the hedge to continue on the other side. This is a favourite hunting ploy of his kind . . . a rapid yet surreptitious approach designed to panic small birds from the cover of the hedge, and the sudden switch designed to catch any panic stricken bird bursting from cover. On this occasion his attack brought no reward and I lost sight of him as he zig-zagged through the birches into the nearby forest.

As a constant background to my meandering, endless skeins of geese criss-crossed the sky — smallish skeins

of greylags, heavier in flight and deeper of voice and larger groups of falsetto pinkfeet, somewhat smaller and, it seemed, more hurried. Rooks and jackdaws added to the general cacophony of noise. A flight of a dozen whoopers added a more musical note.

A covey of partridges rose on whirring wings from the stubble and sped away from my dogs and a gathering of pheasants responded more noisily by rising with loud, throaty protests to clear the spruces and seek a more peaceful place in one of the forest rides.

Another movement caught my eye along the edge of the forest — more menace! It was a dog fox on the prowl. I was downwind of him and quite well camouflaged with the hedge at my back, and so he was completely unaware of me.

He was following a well marked path, no doubt a regular fox highway, and steadily coming straight towards me. His progress was unhurried and unworried although he constantly stopped to sift the air for danger. He also stopped frequently to examine anything and everything, sniffing here and there, perhaps catching the scent of voles in the tussocky grass through which his path took him.

He also marked his progress at frequent intervals, lifting his leg and leaving a succession of visiting cards to inform other foxes of his presence. Foxes are solitary creatures yet there is a social order of vocal contact and scenting.

He rarely moved forward more than a few paces before he stopped again, his sensitive nose providing a never-ending 'computer' read-out of what had passed this way before. His nose did not, however, tell him of the presence of a brown hare some 50 yards away to his right.

As if it knew that there was enough distance between it and the fox, the hare first stood on its hind legs, bolt upright, ears flicking this way and that, nose working overtime, and then loped off at right angles to the path of the fox, quite unconcerned and unhurried.

I was sure the hare was well aware of the presence of the fox, but equally sure that Foxy knew nothing of the hare. Maybe he had picked up the scent but had ignored it knowning that the hare could outrun him anyway and that he would be unprepared to expend energy needlessly in some fruitless chase.

Suddenly, he did pick up an interesting scent for he paused and examined the grass really intently, pushing that black button of a nose deep into a particular tussock. He spent a good half minute examining it then cocked a leg and turned briskly into the cover of the forest and out of sight.

As I now turned homeward, the geese seemed even more active, skeins large and small heading in every direction. The rooks and daws were gathering and heading for their roost and the sun painted the few clouds out to the west in a lovely warm pink glow.

The snow cap on the ben sparkled and the sun dipped to the horizon casting an almost bronzed light across the stubble accentuating the rich colours of the hedgerows and trees.

Snowy landscape tells its own story

SOME years ago now, I lived in close proximity to an ancient and very well used badger sett. And, needless to say, I spent endless hours — usually perched somewhat precariously in a tree — visiting Mr and Mrs Badger and successive generations of their family. My most persistent visits to the sett were, of course, made during the early summer,. Not only did that enable me to watch the young badger families make their first appearance above the ground and subsequently their rapid development as cubs, but it also gave me maximum daylight hours during which to watch them.

Badgers are, for the most part, creatures of the night. But, in May and especially in June, in these northern climes, we enjoy very prolonged hours of daylight and my visits to the sett became, at that time of year, almost a nightly ritual.

However, I did visit the sett at other times of the year. I always found fascination in taking a stroll there after snowfalls to see just how active my neighbourhood badgers had been.

There is a relatively common misconception that badgers hibernate. They don't and indeed they can be quite active even after quite heavy snowfalls. In fact, occasionally I used to encounter badgers late at night in and around my garden but it was after snowfall that I could really plot their movements.

Obviously, they visited my garden quite regularly . . . but usually without my knowing anything about it! Snow cover revealed, through the well - defined tracks, that they were quite regular visitors.

Badgers tend to be creatures of habit — but then so are most mammals. In the case of badgers, however, their tracks are the equivalent of major highways, very distinct and quite wide. Thus it was easy to piece together their nightly travels.

I don't, these days, have a sett in quite such close proximity but there is one which, over the years, I have visited on a fairly regular basis. It isn't as well developed and indeed is only used sporadically.

For some time now, there has been no activity at all but a couple of weeks ago I noticed there were definite signs of a least some traffic. My guess is that it may have been occupied by a lone badger as a winter residence and I will be keeping a watchful eye on it in the hope that activity may increase in the spring.

The one good thing about snow, other than the beauty of a snowy landscape, is that a whole pattern of animal activity can be studied. The slots of roe betray that they too have regular highways and, during the recent snows, I was able to follow some very distinct roe tracks . . . and as a reward, catch up with them . . . as many as a dozen in just an hour's stroll!

There were also the tiny tracks of small animals, mice, voles and even shrews to study . . . and the very distinctive trails of foxes too.

I say distinctive, for apart from the footprints themselves, dog-like but neater and rather more diamond shaped, in ideal conditions the hairs between the toes can also be seen. In addition, the trail itself is virtually

straight, that is to say that the prints are generally in line astern of one another.

Foxes and cats share the facility of being able to place their hind feet in exactly the same spot that the preceding front feet have been, a useful tactic which enables them to concentrate on their quarry and where they place their front feet without having to worry about where their hind feet are going to come down.

I have heard quite a bit. of fox vocalisation in the past couple of weeks as their mating season approaches. The contact calls — the vixen's scream and the triple bark of the dog — have been quite evident and I have also had the joy of watching foxes on their travels twice in the last few days.

My first encounter was brief and merely allowed me to watch a fox speed across a field but my second encounter was lengthier and much more interesting.

She was, by my reckoning, a young vixen and I picked her up as she crossed a road in front of me and entered a field which has not been 'tidied up' and which therefore contains a fair proportion of scrub, birch, whin and broom.

Her progress was unhurried as she loped along in that easy gait so characteristic of a fox which knows there is no immediate threat to it.

She was a fairly leggy beast, her coat brindled red, her fine brush, white tipped. She crossed the open ground at a brisk trot, once breaking into a run as a car on the main road she had just crossed, passed.

She bounded in a zig zag for just a few yards before resuming an easier lope, pausing to test the wind and flex those large, pointed ears as the noise of the car receded and then began to investigate each bush in turn.

Like all foxes, she was looking for any feeding opportunity.

They survive so well because they are not at all fussy about food. They are opportunists.

Each bush prompted a close inspection. On such a bleak day — it was snowing — she no doubt speculated on surprising some small bird sheltering on the lower branches, or a rabbit cowering under the bare branches . . . even perhaps an adventurous vole or mouse emerging from its underground run.

I watched her for a good ten minutes as she turned this way and that, inspecting each shrub and each rank clump of grass. Once she stopped for a full minute to intently examine a clump of grass with her nose. Perhaps there had been another fox this way and perhaps it had left its visiting card.

Such is the communication between foxes. Scent is laid to provide information for other foxes and whilst foxes do hold territories, there is plenty of overlap. Fox highways may be used by several foxes and each must leave notice of its presence!

Now she dipped to leave a trace of her own scent before weaving her way towards the wood. Eventually, she loped off out of sight amongst the trees.

The scent left behind by travelling foxes is distinctive and strongly reminiscent of ammonia. Often I catch a whiff of the smell when out walking and for sure I know that a fox recently passed that way.

For the same reason, it is easy to identify a fox den as distinct from that of a badger. Badgers also leave scent trails but their scent is not quite as strong and musky rather than harsh. And, of course, badgers are exceptionally house proud and meticulously clean.

You will not find food scraps outside a badger sett as you will around a fox earth. Surprisingly, there are occasions when foxes and badgers will share a large sett. I can't imagine that the badgers take too kindly to their untidy neighbours. There are even occasions when badger and fox cubs will play together — something I have never witnessed but something I would love to see.

Each snowfall therefore tells its own stories. It is probably easier after snow to determine just how many animals there are in your patch than at any other time. And although mammals are somewhat elusive normally, you'd be surprised at just how many animals you may have close by without even knowing!

Greater riches to be found

IN recent years there has been a revival of the works of some of those pioneer naturalists upon whose intimate knowledge our own understanding and interest in wildlife, is built.

In particular, I recently acquired a book, published a year or two ago, on the early nineteenth century Scottish based naturalist, Charles St. John. His record of study, especially of birds in Scotland, embellished by his sensitive sketches, makes fascinating reading.

Today, we may know in rather more intimate detail, the life story of a particular bird or animal; indeed the modern naturalist has a plethora of technical gear not only to aid his or her close study of a subject, but the wonder of film and video which such illustrate — to the world at large — even the most intimate passages of real life. Our forebearers, instead of instantly capturing such moments, sat for hour upon hour, sketchbook in hand.

Much as I have come to admire the painstaking work of many such forerunners of the modern naturalist, there was another side to the story which engenders feelings not of admiration but of sadness. For in the pursuit of knowledge, and I'm afraid fame and fortune too, many of the early naturalists were guilty of the destruction of their subject material.

Collector - mania was rife in the nineteenth century. The rise of the nouveau riche was illustrated in the trappings with which they chose to decorate their increasingly ambitious houses, some of which looked more like castles and mansions than real castles and mansions!

Among those trappings, it became fashionable to exhibit mounted specimens of animals and birds; the rarer the bird or animal thus displayed, the greater the prestige to be obtained as a result.

Thus it was that naturalists as well as gamekeepers, shepherds, bailifs and many others, joined in what developed into a wholesale slaughter of some of our most precious birds and animals.

I have written before of the nineteenth century naturalist who apparently risked life and limb in his pursuit of the last pair of kites breeding in England — in the Lake District — by climbing the crags upon which they bred and promptly shooting them! Thus they became a subject for close study on his part, and embellishment perhaps in someone's front hall . . . and part of history. Stuffed birds don't breed!

The modern taxidermist, in the main, works upon a totally different basis, relying upon specimens which have come to grief by accident.

I have used mounted specimens myself to illustrate the beauty of some of our birds and animals to both children and adults and I think such tools are an invaluable aid in the cause that espouses a greater interest in our wildlife.

Polecat

But there is still a sinister side to the story. Charles St. John, on many occasions, raided the nests of birds such as ospreys and robbed them of their eggs . . . repeatedly. He also shot many ospreys so that they too could be possessed by fellow naturalists, or become in their turn, embellishments.

No doubt he made a good living at it! No doubt too that some keepers made a good living by shooting and trapping specimens of various kinds and thereafter selling them.

So much of this kind of activity coincided with the growth of sporting aspects of life in the countryside and, with the rising level of sporting birds reared artificially to provide even better 'sport' a parrallel desire to see that the maximum number of birds presented themselves before the guns.

This engendered a hatred and consequently a wide scale slaughter of any natural predator seen to be a threat.

Thus it was that various estate records from the late nineteenth century and early part of this, show staggering kills of predators of all kinds on many estates. And thus it was that wildcat and pine marten were pushed to the very brink of extinction, polecats totally disappeared as Scottish animals, sea eagles became extinct and ospreys too deserted Scotland as a favoured breeding haunt.

I think it is fair to say that a more enlightened attitude pervades in the countryside now. Television has kindled a new, brightly burning flame of interest in all things natural by allowing arm chair naturalists the pleasure of observing in intimate detail the flora and fauna of not only this country but of the world.

Conservation is a word understood by millions, if not necessarily practised by most of them. Conservation and a real desire in many hearts to defend our heritage has resulted in the growth of countless organisations which, in the field of wildlife, employ modern day naturalists who arm themselves not with guns but with cameras.

But collector mania persists in pockets. Egg collectors still rob nests, and I write not of the little boys who take the eggs of dunnocks or larks, or whatever — an activity to be discouraged in the most vigourous manner — but of those who deliberately set out to steal the eggs of our rarer birds . . . ospreys, goshawks, black throated divers and the like . . . for financial gain or to embellish their own macabre hoards and collections of eggs.

There is still, I understand, a lucrative market for young falcons and this lure of money also jeopardises their future; and there are still those who see predators as a threat to their cossetted sporting birds which are, in any case, destined to be shot and who still carry on a vendetta against them. A pair of eagles was recently found poisoned in the far north so there is still war waged now as it was a hundred years ago.

Thus the emphasis has switched amongst modern day naturalists. Whereas the forebears of today's naturalists, amateur or professional, often themselves killed and collected to advance their own knowledge and perhaps, income, today's naturalists are actively involved in the protection of the creatures at the heart of their interest.

Hundreds — perhaps thousands — of volunteers spend long nightime vigils guarding the nests of ospreys, kites, perigrines and the like in order to defeat those who put their own sordid personal gain before anything else.

What an irony that those of us periodically charged with that kind of responsibility, of protecting ospreys and the like, should owe so much to those early naturalists who, had they been alive and active today, would have earned our scorn and whose collars we would have been glad to see fingered!

A feathered carol singer

MUCH of the wildlife to be witnessed at this time of the year is most easily found marching across our mantelpieces in the form of subject matter for our legions of Christmas cards.

But because this season has been particularly mild — thus in effect shortening the winter — there is still plenty to be seen in the great outdoors.

There is also something rather special in the sounds of the countryside in winters such as this. It isn't just the wild winter sound of the geese as they move relentlessly round the fields; nor is it the straggles of rooks and jackdaws that each morning caw the morning's first beams of sunlight in. I am uplifted by a sweeter sound — some might say an unseasonal sound, one more fitting for the spring that is to come.

For I have heard the first waking song of a thrush. That sweet melody, repeated usually thrice, sometimes four times seems somehow to guarantee the spring which must inevitably follow winter.

I am under no illusion. The winter is not yet past but there is a promise of the days — now at last lengthening — which will herald the birth of a new year.

Whilst the robin's non-stop belling keeps us cheery through even the darkest days of the winter, those first choruses of the mavis are something extra special.

Any keen observer of garden birds will indeed be familiar with the purposeful passage of thrushes. They arrive on a lawn, speckled and round-eyed, in a sudden flurry.

Rock still they stand and then that purposeful hop towards some hidden food store . . . a worm perhaps which betrays itself to them if not to us.

There follows a probing and the inevitable tug of war before the prize is won and thereafter consumed with great delight.

An even greater prize may be found in the shape of snails which still move about our gardens sluggishly. This delectable prey has long been a favourite of the mavis and indeed has prompted the development of a piece of bird technology not yet learned by others.

Watch a thrush seize upon a snail and carry it away to a special place where lies a stone — the thrush's anvil. Here the snail will be smashed to oblivion, its hard shell defence broken by the ingenuity of a bird which has, through the ages, learned to apply the strategy of carefully measured brute force to gain a meal.

With the patience of the smith who carefully fashions a horse shoe on his anvil, the thrush will hammer away at the shell until that defence is undone . . . on an anvil. The same stone is used time and time again, the evidence of many a succulent meal there for all to see in the litter of broken shells.

The success of thrushes is evidenced in their catholic eating habits. At the end of summer, the same birds which delighted in pulling worms from my lawn, descended with great glee on the rich crop of berries borne by the rowans this year.

Any berry-bearing shrub is a target for their avarice. An autumn gathering of thrushes will strip the fruits on a single tree in a matter of minutes.

Those large dark eyes seem somehow to be ever searching for the main chance . . . fruit or insect life, it matters not; they are entirely omnivorous and it sometimes seems, never satisfied in their quest for more and more food.

Nor are they ever still for long. Their never-ending quest for sustenance seems to provide them with a nervous energy that is never exhausted . . . until they pause to sing.

My first mavis song this winter came, ironically enough, from the very heart of the city.

Above the rumble of the traffic and against a background of hurrying shoppers bent on the eternal Christmas quest that sweet music issued from the trees that adorn the gardens below the castle rock of our capital city.

I could not tell if those with whom I shared the pavements were aware of this extra Christmas carolling.

Yet those mellow tones surmounted the traffic's roar; somehow, at least for me, suppressed the feelings of panic that can catch like a fire and hurtle the most casual shopper into the collective frenzy that is Christmas.

The notes were as rounded as any choirboy's; the melody as perfectly pitched as any symphony; the rhythm as constant as that purveyed by the buskers on the pavement.

So for me, the mavis's song is this year's Christmas carol, a natural note struck in opposition to the commercial face sported by the modern Christmas.

It will also be my New Year's overture . . . a hint of kinder, sunnier days to come when the sun begins to climb in the sky and breathe new life into the dormant winter sod from which will spring — eternally — a new cycle and new life. A cheery note that says in spite of it all, it is good to be alive!

Sing on sweet thrush, upon the
leafless bough,
Sing on sweet bird, I listen to thy
strain,
And aged winter, mid his early
reign,
At thy blythe carol, clears his
furrowed brow.
Robert Burns